THE INDEPENDENT GUIDE TO

UNIVERSAL ORLANDO 2017

GIOVANNI COSTA

Limit of Liability and Disclaimer of Warranty: The publisher has used its best efforts in preparing this book, and the information provided herein is provided "as is." Independent Guides and the author make no representation or warranties with respect to the accuracy or completeness of the contents of this book and specifically disclaim any implied warranties of merchantability or fitness for any particular purpose and shall in no event be liable for any loss of profit or any other commercial damage, including but not limited to special, incidental, consequential, or other damages. Please read all signs and safety information before entering attractions, as well as the terms and conditions of any third party companies used. Prices are approximate, and do fluctuate.

Contents

Introduction

In 1971, Orlando was put on the map as the theme park capital of the world with the opening of the Walt Disney World Resort. It was a place that families could visit together to make memories. The resort was a giant version of the Disneyland Resort that had opened in 1955.

Much like Disney, in the late 1980s, Universal announced it too would get in on the thrill game too by opening its own East Coast theme park, similar to the one it had in Hollywood, but on a bigger scale.

Disney saw this new theme park as a big competitor and decided that it would also build a theme park based around movie studios. Miraculously, *Disney's*

MGM Studios managed to open its doors in 1989, before the grand opening of Universal Studios Florida one year later. MGM was a rushed project; and *Universal Studios Florida* blew Disney's theme park away when it opened in 1990.

In 1995, the expansion of Universal Orlando began as the company invested billions of dollars to create a second theme park, *Universal's Islands of Adventure*. Three on-site resort hotels and an entertainment and dining district, *CityWalk*, were also constructed.

The original *Universal Studios Florida* park was also expanded with new areas to create a multi-day destination rivalling Disney.

In 1999, *Universal's Islands of Adventure* opened to rave reviews. It featured innovative attractions such as *The Amazing Adventures of Spider-Man* and *The Incredible Hulk Coaster* that win awards year after year, even to this day.

The Universal Orlando Resort has fast become *the* place to visit in Orlando. Innovative attractions and areas such as *The Simpsons Ride* and *The Wizarding World of Harry Potter*, have sent visitor figures sky-rocketing. Collectively, both theme parks now welcome 16 million guests yearly.

2017 marks an exciting year for the resort with an on-site water park and other new attractions opening.

Tickets

Getting the best Universal Orlando ticket is crucial, and the right choice can save you a lot of money. There are many different ticket options that can be purchased for Universal Orlando. In this section we dissect them all.

Advanced Tickets

Guests from anywhere in the world can buy advanced tickets. The easiest place to purchase these tickets is the official Universal Orlando website at www.universalorlando. com.

There are two types of advanced tickets: a Single Park ticket allows you access to one theme park per day (either to *Universal Studios Florida* or *Islands of Adventure* on any one day), and Park-to-Park tickets allow you to enter both theme parks on the same day.

With multi-day Single Park tickets, you are able to visit the two parks on separate days, but you will not be able to visit both parks on the same day (to do that you need a Park-to-Park ticket).

Single Park tickets allow you to ride every attraction in a single park per day with the exception of the *Hogwarts Express*, which requires a Park-to-Park ticket.

As you will see from the prices below, a single day ticket is expensive on its own. Additional days bring down the 'cost per day' significantly.

You can upgrade any Single Park ticket to a Park-to-Park ticket for an extra $50. You need to decide whether the flexibility of moving between parks on the same day, and access to the *Hogwarts Express* are worth the extra cost.

Child prices apply to children aged 3 to 9 years old. Children under 3 get free admission into the theme parks (proof of age may be requested at the turnstiles). The prices in the grid exclude tax.

Multi-park tickets bought via Universal's website include a book with $150 of coupons. A Universal "convenience fee" of $2.15 is added to online bookings.

Pricing for a 3-Park ticket with Volcano Bay has not yet been released for the US market.

Getting your tickets: Advanced Tickets can be picked up from 'Will Call' kiosks at the theme parks, or printed at home. You can also have tickets mailed to you at an extra cost.

Single Park Tickets:

	1 Day	2 Days	3 Days	4 Days
Adult	$105	$169.99	$179.99	$189.99
Child	$100	$159.99	$169.99	$179.99

Park-to-Park Tickets:

	1 Day	2 Days	3 Days	4 Days
Adult	$155	$219.99	$229.99	$239.99
Child	$150	$209.99	$219.99	$229.99

More on Advanced Purchase Tickets

How much do I save by buying my tickets in advance?

All multi-day tickets are $20 cheaper when pre-purchased online than buying at the park gates (you will be able to see this 'gate' pricing in the next section). So, book online and save yourself some serious cash and time.

The 'Will Call' machines at the front of the park can only be used to pick up advanced tickets. If you have not purchased in advance, you will need to wait in the ticket queue line to see a Team Member and buy your tickets.

You can buy tickets at any on-site hotel and save $20 on tickets compared to park prices. You therefore pay the same price as is charged online.

What about water park access?

At the time of writing, you can add access to 'Wet 'n' Wild' water park which is located a two-minute drive from Universal property. This add-on can be added onto multi-day tickets – one visit is $35 or up to 14 days' entry is $55. Universal will be closing 'Wet 'n' Wild' on 1st January 2017 and will open its own water park later in 2017. Although

no official opening date is available, we anticipate seeing it in late Spring. Ticket prices will be released closer to the time.

Can I add extra days to my ticket later?

Yes. To add extra days onto your park ticket, visit Guest Relations at either park before your last day of admission expires. Here your tickets can be upgraded to add on extra days for the difference in price. For 2-day tickets or longer, extra days are only $10 each – adding an extra day onto a trip can be very affordable.

Are there any more ways to get discounted tickets?

Your work HR department may be part of the Universal Fan Club. Membership is free to companies. HR can register by emailing fan club@ universalorlando.com - you will benefit from slightly discounted tickets and other offers.

In addition, there are other websites and ticket brokers that offer tickets at reduced prices. We recommend you thoroughly check the reputation of the website you are purchasing from if you do not order from the official Universal

website. Avoid second-hand sales. One large ticket broker is UndercoverTourist.com.

Do international visitors get a discount?

United Kingdom residents usually visit Orlando for longer than Americans. Therefore, Universal offers special, longer Universal Bonus and Explorer Tickets. These can also be bought online outside the UK in some locations, but they are harder to find.

A 2-park Bonus Ticket with access to both Universal theme parks for 14 consecutive days is priced at £159 for adults and £152 for children in 2016. A 3-Park Bonus ticket with access to both Universal parks (plus Wet 'n Wild) for 14 consecutive days is £171 for adults and £163 for children.

The 2017 price for a 2-Park Explorer Ticket is £223 per adult and £215 per child. A 3-park ticket (with access to Volcano Bay Water Park from 1 June 2017) is the same price as the 2-Park ticket for 2017.

These tickets are also sold at brokers such as www.attraction-tickets-direct.co.uk and www.attractiontix.co.uk.

Gate Price Tickets

If you do not purchase your tickets in advance, you will need to buy them at the theme park ticket booths. These are "gate price" tickets, and are the most expensive.

One day tickets vary in price at the gate depending on the visit date - they are always the same price online. Multi-day tickets are $20 more at the theme park than online.

In addition to paying over the odds, you will waste valuable vacation time by waiting in a queue line instead of enjoying the theme parks.

As you are clearly planning your Universal Orlando visit in advance, there is no need to pay for a gate price ticket.

Top Tip: A disability discount of 15% off the gate price is available at the resort from Guest Services. Anyone who feels they cannot experience the attractions in the park perhaps due to fear or height requirements can also get this discount.

No proof of disability is required but abuse this discount could mean it being withdrawn. Some tickets will still be cheaper online than at the park price with this discount.

Single Park Tickets:

	1 Day	2 Days	3 Days	4 Days
Adult	$119	$189.99	$199.99	$209.99
Child	$114	$179.99	$189.99	$199.99

Park-to-Park Tickets:

	1 Day	2 Days	3 Days	4 Days
Adult	$169	$239.99	$249.99	$259.99
Child	$164	$229.99	$239.99	$249.99

Orlando Flextickets

The Orlando Flexticket includes entry into both Universal Orlando resort theme parks as well, as SeaWorld Orlando, Aquatica Water Park and Wet 'n Wild Water Park for 14 consecutive days. It also includes free access to select live entertainment venues at Universal Orlando's CityWalk complex (visitors must be 21 or older for some venues).

Another benefit of the ticket is that you only pay for parking once each day, regardless of the number of parks visited; simply show the parking receipt from first park visited that day when going to other parks.

2016 pricing for the Orlando Flexticket is $369.95 per adult, and $354.95 per child. 2017 pricing is yet to be released.

In addition, the Orlando Flexticket Plus option for sale includes access to the five aforementioned parks plus Busch Gardens Tampa Bay for the same period of 14 consecutive days. 2016 pricing for the Orlando Flexticket Plus is $389.95 per adult, and $374.95 per child.

Both Flexticket options can be purchased from www.universalorlando.com or from a number of ticket brokers. UK visitors can get this ticket from brokers too.

Florida Resident Tickets

Florida Residents can take advantage of discounts on multi-day tickets. Proof of residency must be shown when picking up tickets and/or when entering the turnstiles.

Florida residents planning on visiting for more than 3 days in a year should strongly consider Universal Orlando's annual passes.

A valid Florida ID must be shown for each ticket purchased when picking them up. Accepted IDs are:
• Florida driver's license
• Florida state-issued ID card (must have Florida address)
• Florida voter's registration card with corresponding photo ID
• College ID from a Florida college or university with corresponding photo ID

Florida Resident tickets are valid for up to 60 days, so you have added flexibility as to when you can visit.

Florida Resident discounted tickets must be purchased online in advance and collected at any ticket window at both theme parks; these tickets cannot be purchased at the gates.

Blackout dates apply to Florida resident tickets. December 17th, 2016 to December 31st, 2016. 2017 blockout dates were not available at the time of writing.

Florida Resident Single Park Tickets:

	1 Day	2 Days	3 Days
Adult	$105	$149.99	$159.99
Child	$100	$140.99	$150.99

Florida Resident Park-to-Park Tickets:

	1 Day	2 Days	3 Days
Adult	$155	$189.99	$199.99
Child	$150	$180.99	$190.99

Florida Resident Annual Passes

Florida residents can get discounts on annual passes. Pricing is as follows: Seasonal pass - $259.99, Power Pass - $319.99 plus tax; Preferred Pass - $349.99 plus tax; and Premier Pass - $484.99 plus tax.

Put simply, the features of these passes are exactly the same as the non-Florida resident annual passes mentioned on the next page, except Florida residents pay less for their passes.

Proof of residency must be shown when picking up the Florida resident annual pass and/or when entering the turnstiles.

A valid Florida ID must be shown for each annual pass purchased.

Annual Passes

Annual passes allow you to visit the resort as often as you wish (subject to blackout dates on some passes) at a very low per-visit price. In addition, special perks are offered to Passholders, including discounts on dining and merchandise. There are four types of annual pass. Discover them all below.

	Seasonal Pass	Power Pass	Preffered Pass	Premier Pass
Pricing (for guests of all ages - excludes tax)	$284.99	$344.99	$384.99	$539.99
One Year of Unlimited Park-to-Park Admission	Blockout dates apply.	Blockout dates apply.	Yes	Yes
Free self-parking (after 1st visit)	No	50% off	Yes	Yes
Free valet and preferred self-parking (after first visit)	No	No	No	Yes
Discounts on theme park and special event tickets	Yes	Yes	Yes	Yes
One free Halloween Horror Nights ticket (Sun to Thurs)	No	No	No	Yes
Free admission to select special events (e.g. Mardi Gras)	No	Yes	Yes	Yes
Discounted food & merchandise	No	No	Yes	Yes
Discount on Blue Man tickets	Yes	Yes	Yes	Yes
Free CityWalk club access	No	No	No	Yes
Discounts at on-site hotels	Yes	Yes	Yes	Yes
Free Universal Express Pass (after 4:00pm)	No	No	No	Yes

Blockout dates for the Power Pass and Seasonal Pass:
These passes have dates that are blocked out (i.e. can't enter the parks).

• December 17th 2016 to 3rd January 17th - Both passes blocked out
• 8th April 2017 to 22nd April 2017 - Both passes blocked out.

• 10th June 2017 to 13th August 2017 - Seasonal Pass blocked out.
• 21st December 2017 to 31st December 2017 - Both passes blocked out.
All dates are inclusive.

Top Tip: If you are planning two multi-day visits to the resort within a period of 365 days, then an annual pass can be a real bargain. If you go one year in July and the next year in June, for example, then the second year's visits will effectively cost almost nothing.

Hotels

Deciding where you stay while on vacation is an important: you must consider price, availability, size, location and amenities in order to find the perfect accommodation for you. Luckily, central Florida is renowned for having an incredible range of options to suit all tastes and budgets.

There are numerous hotels not located on Universal property that are more reasonably priced than the on-site options. However, for the full Universal Orlando experience, we recommend staying at one of the on-site hotels. You will be just minutes away from the action, and the benefits of staying on-site more than make up for the extra cost.

There are **three tiers** of on-site hotels:
• Prime Value – *Cabana Bay Beach Resort*
• Preferred – *Royal Pacific Resort* and *Sapphire Falls Resort*
• Premier – *Portofino Bay Hotel* and *Hard Rock Hotel*

Benefits available to on-site hotel guests:
• Early entry to *The Wizarding World of Harry Potter* one hour before the park opens to regular guests.
• Complimentary water taxis, shuttle buses or walking paths to both parks and Universal *CityWalk*.
• Complimentary delivery of merchandise purchased throughout the resort to your hotel.
• Resort-wide charging privileges. Give your credit card number at check-in to use your room key to charge purchases instead of your card. At check-out, you will settle the balance as one amount.
• Complimentary Super Star Shuttle scheduled transportation to *SeaWorld* and *Aquatica*. This runs once a day from your hotel, and once or twice a day back to your hotel. Seats are reserved at concierge.
• Optional wake-up call from a Universal character.
• Use of the Golf Universal Orlando program.

Guests at *Royal Pacific Resort, Portofino Bay Hotel,* and *Hard Rock Hotel* enjoy these added benefits:
• FREE Universal Express Pass - Unlimited ride access to skip the regular lines in both theme parks all day.
• Priority seating at select restaurants throughout both theme parks and *CityWalk*.

Staying On-Site

In this section we cover all the essentials at staying at any of the five on-site Universal Orlando hotels. From parking to pet rooms, and transportation to toning up.

Parking:
For all Preferred and Premier hotels parking is charged at $20 per night for self-parking and $27 per night for valet parking (plus tips). Hotel guests pay full price for parking, with no discounts.

Day guests who park in the hotel lots pay $22 per day, unless eating in one of the on-site restaurants where they can have their parking validated for up to 3 hours of complimentary parking.

Parking charges at *Cabana Bay Beach Resort* (in the Prime Value hotel category) are $12 per night for hotel guests. Day guests will be charged according to their length of stay.

OFF-SITE ACCOMMODATION

This guide does not cover off-site accommodation. However, if you do decide to stay off-site, we would recommend an apartment rental through Airbnb. There are many places that are a short drive from the park but with all the facilities of a suite - such as a kitchen. Using our exclusive link you can get a discount of at least $25 (and up to $50): www.airbnb.co.uk/c/gdacosta16

FITNESS AND POOLS

Fitness Suites:
All five on-site hotels have complimentary fitness suites for their guests.

Although not widely advertised, guests staying at any on-site hotel can use any of the fitness suites.

This means that a guest from *Cabana Bay Beach Resort* could, for example, visit the gym at the *Hard Rock Hotel* with their room key.

Pools:
All the on-site hotels have impressive pools; even more impressively, you can pool hop. Like the fitness suites mentioned above, if you are staying at any on-site resort hotel you can use the pool of any resort. A fantastic benefit!

Who wouldn't want to try the fun pools at *Cabana Bay*, the magnificent one at the *Hard Rock*, and then finish the day with a dip at the new *Sapphire Falls* pool?

Internet Access:
In-room "standard" Wi-Fi access is complimentary. If you require higher speed access, there is a "premium" option available for $15 per day. The lobby and pool areas at all the on-site hotels have free Wi-Fi, which you can access regardless of whether you are staying at the hotel or not.

Refrigerators:
Refrigerators are not included in the price of rooms at *Royal Pacific Resort*, *Portofino Bay Hotel*, and *Hard Rock Hotel*. They can be rented at the price of $15 per night each, plus tax. Those requiring refrigerators for medical conditions may be able to get a discount or the entire cost waived.

Guests staying at *Cabana Bay Beach Resort*'s family suites, and standard rooms at *Sapphire Falls Resort* have refrigerators included in the nightly room rate.

Pet rooms:
Pet rooms are available at all Premier and Preferred hotels, although an extra cleaning fee is required of $50 per night, up to a maximum of $150 per room.

Character Dining:
The *Royal Pacific Resort, Portofino Bay Hotel,* and *Hard Rock Hotel* offer character-dining experiences where characters visit your table for you to meet, chat and take photographs, while you dine.

At *Portofino Bay Hotel*, this is at *Trattoria del Porto*, at *Hard Rock Hotel* this is at *The Kitchen*, and at the *Royal Pacific Resort* you will find this at the *Islands Dining Room*.

Characters vary from Scooby Doo to Shrek and even the Minions from Despicable Me.

Character dining usually takes place once or twice a week between 6:30pm and 9:30pm. You can visit any resort's restaurant, even if you are not sleeping there.

Kids Activities:
These are available at *Royal Pacific Resort, Portofino Bay Hotel,* and *Hard Rock Hotel* in the evenings. This keeps kids occupied while parents spend quality time together. Guests from any hotel can use the Kids Activities at other hotels. Details can be obtained from the concierge desk. Prices are about $15 an hour.

ON-SITE TRANSPORTATION

At the Preferred or Premier level hotels, your transportation options to each the theme park include: shuttle buses, water taxis, rickshaws and walking paths.

We do not recommend the shuttle buses as you won't save time as the drop-off point is a 10-minute walk from the theme parks.

The water taxis are our preferred form of transportation here, or simply walking. Water taxis begin operating from the hotels 30 minutes before Early Park Admission. The last departure from *CityWalk* is at 2:30am year-round.

The rickshaws are the quickest and most direct way to get around. These are approved by Universal and man-powered and have no set fee, simply tip what you think is appropriate ($2-$4 per person is customary).

At *Cabana Bay* you can use the walking path or shuttle buses. The buses drop you off a 10-minute walk from the parks; the walking path route takes 20 to 25 minutes.

The shuttle buses run every 10 to 15 minutes at all on-site hotels. They are even more frequent at *Cabana Bay*.

Cabana Bay Beach Resort

This 900-room, 900-suite, Retro 1950s and 1960s Prime Value hotel is the most affordable on-site. There are walking paths to the parks and CityWalk (20 to 25 minutes) or you can use the complimentary shuttle.

Room size: Standard rooms are 300 ft² and family suites are 430 ft².
Room prices: $129 to $214, plus tax for a standard room. Family suites are priced at $161 to $284, plus tax.
Activities: A 10-lane bowling alley; arcade room; two resort pools – one with a water slide; s'mores fire pit; hot hub; poolside movies and activities; a store; and a fitness center.

We were astounded on our first visit to *Cabana Bay Beach Resort*. It is a very well themed resort in a 1950s and 1960s style, and it has a fun feeling about it. There are also a wealth of things to do at the most affordable on-site property.

You can easily spend several days just exploring all the amenities on offer, and despite the fact this is a large hotel, the amenities never felt overcrowded to us.

We like the two sizes of rooms, and feel that they are reasonably priced for the location and amenities you get. Standard rooms sleep up to 4 guests, and family suites sleep up to 6.

Even though this resort is significantly cheaper than the others, every room includes all the amenities you would expect: an LCD TV, an in-room safe, a coffee maker, an iron and a hair-dryer. Suites also include a kitchenette area with a microwave, mini-fridge and sink. We were also particularly appreciative of all the plug sockets in the standard rooms and suites, including a multitude of USB sockets!

The resort's Table Service restaurant is part of the bowling alley (more on this later), though you are a short shuttle bus journey away from *CityWalk,* or you can walk to one of the other on-site hotels if you desire something more upscale.

Other food options include a large food court and food trucks outside. In-room pizza delivery is also available.

Perhaps the biggest surprise is the exceptional entertainment on offer: the 10-lane bowling alley is unheard of at any other hotel ($15 per game, shoe rental $4 per pair, and food is available).

Many other amenities that are more commonly found at higher-priced resorts are available here too - and they are all complimentary.

There are two pools at the resort. The main pool at 10,000 ft² has a water slide, and the smaller 8000 ft² pool has as a sandy beach. Both pools offer accessible zero-entry access. The smaller pool even has a lazy river going around it spanning 700 feet.

Free poolside activities happen throughout the day, and there are even s'mores pits to use.

Self-service laundry is available for $3 per wash and $3 per dryer load. Parking is $12 per night for self-parking, payable at check-in.

There are, however, a few downsides to this resort: guests staying at *Cabana Bay* do NOT receive complimentary Express Passes like thy

do at some other on-site hotels; this is usually cited as one of the main reasons for staying on-site.

The price difference between this hotel and those that do include Express Pass is huge, so this is understandable.

There is also no water taxi service to this hotel - it is the only on-site hotel not to have this feature. However, *Cabana Bay* still have the option of walking paths to the resort (up to 25 minutes' walk), as well as continuous, complimentary shuttle bus transportation.

Cabana Bay is currently being expanded with two new towers housing 400 additional guest rooms, opening in 2017. While this is good news for those looking to stay at the most affordable on-site resort, we hope the additional guests will not put strain on the current amenities.

Overall, for those on a budget, but wanting the benefits of staying on-site, Cabana Bay is the best option for you.

DINING:

Bayline Diner – Quick Service food court. Entrées priced at $7 to $8.50 for breakfast, and $6 to $12.50 for lunch and dinner.

Galaxy Bowl Restaurant – Table Service dining and Quick Service food available too. Open from 11:00am to 10:00pm. Entrées priced at $6 to $10.

Atomic Tonic – Poolside bar with drinks and limited snacks. Cocktails $9 to $13.

The Hideaway Bar & Grill – Poolside Bar and grilled fare.

Swizzle Lounge – Bar. Cocktails priced at $9 to $11. Other drinks from $6.

Starbucks – Quick Service location. Sells drinks and snacks at standard prices. Expect to pay $4-$6 per item.

Loews Sapphire Fall Resort

This 1000-room, 83-suite, hotel is the second least expensive on-site resort. It is in the Preferred category and is Caribbean inspired in design.

Transport: Water taxis, pedicabs, walking paths (15 to 20 minutes) and shuttle buses.
Room size: Standard rooms are 364 ft^2, and suites start at 529 ft^2.
Room prices: $179 to $284, plus tax for a standard room.
Activities: A large pool, two white sand beaches, a hot tub, children's water play area with pop jets, and a water slide; fire pit for s'mores; complimentary fitness center for guests including a dry sauna; arcade game room; and a Universal Store.

The newest on-site resort is a beautiful, tropical destination. It provides a step up from *Cabana Bay* in terms of amenities and theming.

The centerpiece of the resort is the 16,000ft^2 pool, the largest in Orlando, as well as the two sandy beaches, and water slide. Pool-side cabanas are available.

Standard rooms sleep up to five people – a roll-away bed is needed at $25 per night. There is also a 115,000 square foot convention space for business travelers.

Note: This hotel does not include Express Passes, and guests do not receive priority seating at restaurants. Both perks are reserved for the more expensive hotels that follow.

DINING:

New Dutch Trading Co. – With ready to go meals, beverages, fresh-baked breads and homemade jams, this is the stop for provisions and supplies. Food is $9 to $12.
Strong Water Tavern – A wall of vintage rums, a ceviche bar and a patio overlooking the lagoon make Strong Water Tavern a unique watering hole. Serving lunch and dinner, with daily rum tastings, this lounge is a destination. Drinks & tapas are $6 to $16 each.
Amatista Cookhouse – Caribbean cuisine prepared in an exhibition kitchen. Whether dining indoors or out, or in one of the private dining areas, guests will feel welcomed and relaxed in this inspiring restaurant. Entrées are $12 to $20.
Drhum Club Kantine – Pool bar serving a Tapas-style menu. Food is $9 to $23, drinks start from $7.

Loews Royal Pacific Resort

This 1000-room, Preferred category hotel is themed to a tropical paradise. A standard room is 335ft². Water taxis, pedicabs, walking paths and buses are available to the parks.

Room prices: $244 to $424 per night, plus tax

Activities: One very large pool, volleyball court, kids' water play area, fitness center, croquet, poolside activities, a torch lighting ceremony, and Wantilan Luau dinner show.

From the moment you step inside, you are a world away from the hustle and bustle of Orlando's theme parks. Yet, they are conveniently located right next door.

There is one large pool at this hotel, a complimentary gymnasium with a variety of cardio and free weight equipment, as well as steam and sauna facilities and a whirlpool.

"Dive-In movies" are screened by the pool on select nights, and pool-side cabanas are available from $100 per day.

On Friday and Saturday nights (and Tuesdays during the peak summer season) guests can enjoy the 'Torch Lighting Ceremony' with hula dancers and fire jugglers by the pool. There is no charge to watch this.

An on-site coin-operated laundry is also available.

DINING:

Orchid Court Lounge and Sushi Bar – Continental breakfast, and sushi bar. Breakfast entrées are $9 to $10. Bar entrées are $12 to $20.

Islands Dining Room – Table Service. Breakfast buffet or a la Carte available. The buffet is priced at $19.50 per adult and $10 per child. All day menu entrées are $16 to $30.

Jake's American Bar – Bar, with light snacks and larger meals. Entrées are $10 to $30.

Bula Bar and Grille – Poolside bar and dining. Entrées are $11 to $15.

Emeril's Tchoup Chop – Signature Table Service. Entrées are $12 to $18 at lunch, and $24 to $30 at dinner.

Wantilan Luau – Hawaiian dinner show starting at 5:00pm or 6:00pm on Saturdays (and Tuesdays during peak season). Reservations required. Buffet including non-alcoholic and select alcoholic drinks; priced at $63 to $70 for adults, and $35 to $40 for children.

Hard Rock Hotel Orlando

This rock 'n' roll, Premier tier, hotel has a mere 650 rooms, including 33 suites. It is the second most expensive hotel on-site, and the closest to the parks.

Transport: Water taxis, pedicabs, walking paths (5 minutes to *Universal Studios Florida* and 10 minutes to *Islands of Adventure*) and shuttle buses.

Room size: 375 ft² for a standard room

Room prices: $289 to $494 per night, plus tax

Activities: Pool, Jacuzzis, poolside movies, volleyball court, and a fitness center

You will feel like rock 'n' roll royalty with impeccable accommodation, a wealth of recreation options, and personal service and attention fit for an "A-List" celebrity at the *Hard Rock Hotel*; the hotel is lively, yet laid back.

Rock fans will love seeing over $1 million of music-related memorabilia throughout the hotel. Classy, yet totally casual, this is a true deluxe hotel.

The highlight of the hotel is the huge 12,000ft² pool, which features zero entry leveling and white sand. It even has an underwater sound system and a slide!

The area also has a beach with a volleyball court and lounge chairs. There are two Jacuzzis, including one that is designated for adults use only.

Most nights there is a "dive-in movie" by the pool, and there are occasionally dive-in

concerts too. Poolside orders from the bar are available.

Cabanas can be rented from $80 to $200 per day, depending on the location of the cabana and the season. Cabanas include soft drinks and bottled water, a TV, fresh fruit, towels and a refrigerator.

Inspired by its *Hard Rock* name, there is a lot of extra musical entertainment offered at this resort hotel. For example, DJ lessons are held daily during peak seasons in the lobby.

What's more if you are a guitar fan, you will love the fact that you can rent out a Fender by AXE guitar at no extra cost during your stay, though a $1000 refundable deposit is required.

Laundry is priced at $3 per wash and $3 per dryer load.

This hotel is the closest to *CityWalk* and the theme parks, being located right next door to *Universal Studios Florida*. This makes hopping back for a dip in the pool in the middle of the day a real possibility.

Top Tip: Look for the plaques next to the musical memorabilia scattered throughout the hotel; each of these has a unique number on it. Call (407) 503-2233 and enter the number on the plaque to learn more about the item you are looking at.

Velvet Sessions – The Ultimate Cocktail Party: From January to October, on the last Thursday of each month you can enjoy Velvet Sessions. The event is described as "a rock & roll cocktail party held in the hotel's Velvet Bar and Lobby Lounge."

Each "Session" showcases a different type of beverage theme for members to sip, shoot or guzzle along with fabulous and great live music from the nation's best rock bands.

Tickets are $29 in advance from www.velvetsessions.com or $35 on the door. VIP tickets are $50. Each ticket includes: Complimentary specialty drinks, finger foods and warm-up tunes, starting at 6:30pm until show time at 8:30pm. There is also a cash bar. After the band performs, stick around for a DJ set until 1:00am. Ages 21 and up only. Past performers include: Brett Michaels, Joan Jett, The Tubes, Blue Oyster Cult, ABC and Foreigner to name but a few.

DINING:

The Palm Restaurant – Table Service dining, steak house. Entrées priced at $12 to $60.
Velvet Bar – Bar with light snacks and bigger plates too. Entrées priced at $12 to $36.
The Kitchen – Buffet at breakfast. Table Service dining at lunch and dinner. Entrées priced at $11 to $37.
Emack & Bolio's – Ice creams, pizzas and small bites. Entrées are $9 to $23.
BeachClub – Bar and Quick Service snacks.

Reservations for Table Service dining establishments can be made at OpenTable.com

Loews Portofino Bay Hotel

Portofino Bay is the best example of what a Premier level luxury resort should be. This 750-room hotel is incredibly well-themed to a small Italian fishing village.

Transport: Water taxis, pedicabs, walking paths and shuttle buses.
Room size: 450 ft² for a standard room
Room prices: $304 to $494 per night, plus tax
Activities: 3 pools, poolside movies, spa (paid), live music.

This premier hotel recreates the charm and romance of the seaside village of Portofino, Italy, right down to the cobblestone streets and cafes.

This is the most luxurious on-site hotel, and the theming is truly mind-blowing.

Families who want a fun addition to their rooms, may want to consider one of the 18 Despicable Me themed Kids Suites with a separate bedroom for the kids.

The hotel has 3 pools. The Beach Pool has a waterslide and the Villa Pool has a Jacuzzi-style area; and the Hillside Pool is the quietest and the most relaxing, with a view along the Bay. On Saturdays, during peak seasons, there is a "Dive-In Movie" for guests to enjoy.

Pool cabanas are available for hire at the Beach Pool and the Villa Pool for those wanting to live the real luxurious lifestyle – these include overhead fans, a TV, and a mini refrigerator stocked with water and soft drinks, and complimentary fruit. Prices start at $75 per day.

The **Mandara Spa**, a brand synonymous with luxury treatments, is located by the beach and offers a variety of indulgent experiences.

The most basic 50-minute Swedish massage starts at $130, and you can expect to pay up to $595 for the "Nirvana...Bliss for a Day" experience that lasts over 6 hours. Facials, body therapies, nail services, waxing and haircuts are also available. Taxes and a 20% service charge are not included.

Any treatment purchased also includes full use of the spa and fitness facilities. On-site guests get free fitness

club access. A fitness day pass can also be purchased for $25 for non-hotel guests. Reservations can be made by calling 407-503-1244.

There is no coin operated guest laundry at this hotel. You can either use the hotel's laundry service or use a self-laundry service at the *Hard Rock Hotel*.

We would advise taking the water taxi from this hotel to the theme parks. The walking path is also a lovely alternative: it is a 20-minute walk.

In the evenings, weather permitting, the *Portofino Bay Hotel* piazza has live music and classical singers, and guests can enjoy the Italian atmosphere.

At **Family Art**

Photography you can get a complimentary family photo-shoot; this can be a classic family portrait, poolside or even underwater. Sessions last 15 to 30 minutes. The session is free, but the prints are the standard prices for this type of work. One 8"x10" print costs about $30, and four 6x6 metallic gloss finish prints will set you back $184, for example. Two 11"x14" canvases cost $194. A DVD of your entire shoot will set you back $375, excluding tax. You can also order from home at www.familyartonline.com.

Harbor Nights:

Four times per year, the Portofino Bay Resort hosts 'Harbor Nights', a wine tasting and jazz event designed to capture the ambiance of the Mediterranean. Each event features select wines, gourmet food, live music and other live entertainment.

Pricing is usually $45 per person in advance, or $55 on the door (subject to availability). A VIP seating option is priced at $75. All prices exclude tax. There is even a Holiday edition with a tree-lighting ceremony.

DINING:

Bice – Table Service gourmet dining. Entrées are priced at $19 to $48.
The Thirsty Fish Bar – Bar with light snacks. Open from 6:00pm.
Trattoria del Porto – Table Service dining. Entrées are priced at $9 to $18 at breakfast, and start at $9 for lunch and dinner.
Mama Della's Ristorante – Family style Italian cuisine.
Sal's Market Deli – Quick Service. Serves sandwiches, paninis and pizzas.
Gelateria Caffe Espresso – Coffees and ice creams priced at $3 to $7.
Bar American – Upscale bar, also serves food. Open from 4:00pm to 11:00pm. Entrées are $15 to $16. Small bites are $10 to $14.
Splendido Pizzeria – Pizza, salads and sandwiches. Entrées are $13 to $18.

Reservations for Table Service dining establishments can be made at OpenTable.com

Getting There

Before we get too carried away with all the fun you can have at the Universal Orlando Resort, you must first make your way there.

By Car

Universal Orlando Resort is located 10 miles southwest of the city of Orlando, Florida and about 10 miles northeast of the Walt Disney World Resort. Universal Orlando can be reached easily by car from the Interstate 4 (I-4), and following Universal Blvd north to the parking garages. The address for your GPS is 6000 Universal Blvd, Orlando, FL.

The parking garages accommodate 20,000 vehicles, so be sure to remember where you park. They open at least 90 minutes before park opening time and all levels except the top level are covered.

Top Tip: When approaching the parking toll plaza, stay in the leftmost lane – most people go to the right; this can save 5 to 10 minutes on busy days.

There is an easy to remember parking system: each parking spot is assigned a character name and a number. Note it down!

Also, take a photo of your parking location (but also write it down in case your battery dies). The parking garages are located are a 5 to 10-minute walk from the theme parks.

Parking is $20 per day for self-parking (free for Preferred and Premier Passholders). Preferred parking is $25 (discounted for Preferred Passholders, free for Premier Passholders) and valet is $35 a day ($15 for Preferred Passholders, free for Premier Passholders). "Red carpet valet" is $10 extra, and you get your car within 5 minutes.

Disabled parking bays can be requested. These are closer to *CityWalk* and the theme parks.

Lunchtime visitors to *CityWalk* can get free valet parking by validating their restaurant receipt from Monday to Friday for two hours of free parking. Ask your restaurant for the hours of this offer. A passenger drop-off point is also available.

Between 6:00pm and 10:00pm parking is $5 (free for Florida residents with proof of residency). After 10:00pm, parking is free for all guests. On peak evenings, like Halloween Horror Nights, parking is full price all day.

After parking, you walk to the main parking hub, pass security screening and walk through *CityWalk* – then turn left for *Islands of Adventure* or right for *Universal Studios Florida*.

Disney to Universal Orlando by car:
You will first need to follow internal Disney resort signs to the Interstate 4 (I-4). There are entrances to the I-4 by *ESPN: Wide World of Sports, Disney's Pop Century Resort, Disney's Typhoon Lagoon water park,* and *Disney Springs.*

Follow the I-4 North/East for 6 to 8 miles, take exit 75A and merge onto Universal Blvd.

Shuttles Services

There is no free Universal transportation between the Universal Orlando Resort and Orlando International Airport.

We have found Mears and Super Shuttle reliable, though other services are available. Prices are $30 to $35 per person return, or about $20 one-way.

Disney to Universal Orlando by shuttle: A Super Shuttle quote for this route is about $45 for a 4-seater for a one-way trip, plus tip. A taxi is cheaper.

Taxis

We recommend a taxi if coming to the Universal Orlando Resort from the airport without a car, especially if in a group.

The cost is usually about $55-70 with a tip each way. Mears Transportation offers a taxi service and we have found them, to be reliable, though others are available.

Disney to Universal Orlando by taxi: A quote is about $35 for a taxi from Epcot to Universal, excluding tip. UberX is $20 to $35.

Public Transportation

There are two public transportation options: I-Ride Trolley and Lynx buses. The I-Ride follows a route along International Drive aimed at tourists; Lynx is a public bus system.

Both services stop just outside *Wet 'n' Wild Water Park*. From there it is a 20-minute walk to the Universal area, crossing a few major roads.

From the bus stop, cross the road and head north on Universal Blvd towards the theme parks until you reach the overhead walkway, which you will use to enter Universal Orlando. Both options are about

$2 each.

Disney to Universal Orlando: Go to the *Transportation and Ticket Center (TTC)* on Disney property; for most guests this means going to *Magic Kingdom Park* and taking the monorail to the *TTC*.

At the *TTC*, ask or the location of the LYNX bus stop. Alternatively, catch the Lynx bus at *Disney Springs* – use Google Maps to locate this stop.

At either stop, catch the number 50 LYNX bus. Ask for a transfer ticket when paying. Ride the Number 50 bus for about 35 minutes until the first stop on Sea

Harbor Drive. The exact stop location is 6800 Sea Harbor Dr and Central Florida Pky.

Here you will wait for the number 8 LYNX bus and stay on that bus until 6200 International Dr and Universal Blvd. The number 8 bus journey will take about 15 minutes.

From here, it is a 20-minute walk to the Universal Orlando Resort. The journey time with transfers is about 1h15m to 1h30m each way.

If you have a smartphone, use Google Maps to plan this route; buses are not regular.

Universal Studios Florida

*Universal Studios Florid*a opened in 1990 as the Floridian cousin to the popular Universal Studios theme park in Hollywood. The original idea of the park was to experience how movies are made. Actual filming would be done in the park too. Over the years the focus of the park has changed slightly and the philosophy is now to ride and "experience the movies" for yourself, rather than seeing how they are made. The park hosted 9.6 million guests in 2015.

Note: Average attraction waits noted in this section here are estimates for busy summer days when on school break. Wait times may well be lower at other times of the year. They may also occasionally be higher, especially during the week of 4th July, Thanksgiving, Christmas, New Year and other public holidays.

Where we list food prices, this information was accurate during our last visit to the restaurant. We also do not post the full menu but just a sample of the food on offer. Meal prices listed do not include a drink, unless otherwise stated. When an attraction is listed as requiring lockers, all loose items must be stored in complimentary lockers outside each attraction.

Attraction Key

In the next two chapters, we list each attraction individually along with some key information. Here are what the symbols in the next sections mean.

 Does it have Express Pass?

 Minimum height (in inches)

 Is there an On-Ride Photo?

 Ride/Show Length

 Average wait times (on peak days)

 Do I need to place my belongings in a locker before riding?

Production Central

Production Central is the gateway to Universal Studios Florida. You must pass through it to get to the rest of the park; it contains shops and a number of attractions.

Production Central is home to **Guest Services** is located where you can request disability passes, make dining reservations, ask questions, provide positive feedback and make complaints. You can also exchange some currencies at this location. It is located to the right after the turnstiles. To the left of the turnstiles you will find **lockers**, as well as **stroller** and **wheelchair rentals**.

The **Studio Audience Center** (to the right after the turnstiles) is the place to get tickets for shows being filmed in the soundstages at Universal. Tickets are complimentary. This is also the location for **Lost and Found**.

First Aid is located next to the Studio Audience Center. Another First Aid station is located next to Louie's Italian Restaurant.

You will also find the **American Express Passholder Lounge** in this area of the park, opposite the Shrek shop. This lounge is reserved for those who use an AmEx card to buy park tickets or an annual pass. Inside the lounge you will find bottled water, snacks and phone charging facilities. Simply show your ticket receipt, the ticket itself, and your AmEx card for entry. Guests who use an AmEx card for in-park purchases but do not use it to purchase their park tickets, do not have access to this lounge.

If you need to mail something, you can drop off your letters and postcards at the **mailbox**, located to the left as you come in after the turnstiles, to the right of the lockers. **Stamps** can be bought from the On Location shop here on the Front Lot. **Calling cards** can be bought from a vending machine near the **lockers**.

Family & Health Services, which includes a nursing room, is located to the right after the turnstiles.

Attractions

Despicable Me: Minion Mayhem

✄ Yes   40"   📷 No   ⌄ 4 minutes   🔒 No   ⏳ 60 to 120 minutes

A simulator ride featuring 4D effects. 'Despicable Me' fans will be very excited, but others may miss some of the cuteness. Due to the low hourly capacity and the popularity of its characters, queues are almost always lengthy.

Top Tip: A stationary version of this attraction operates at select times where you sit in benches at the front of the theater. These do not move, but you get the 3D experience. When this is offered, the wait time is usually short, e.g. 10 minutes versus 90 minutes. There is a separate queue line for this.

Fun Fact: The trees outside the ride are banana trees, as the minions love the fruit!

Shrek 4-D

✄ Yes   None   📷 No   ⌄ 12 minutes   ⏳ 15 to 45 minutes   🔒 No

Stepping into Shrek 4D, you know you are getting into a different kind of attraction – it is not just a 3D, but a 4D experience. The unique part of this attraction is the seats, which act like personal simulators. For those not wishing to experience the seat movement, a limited number of stationary seats are also available. The movie is great fun with some corny jokes and jabs at Disney thrown in too,

Hollywood Rip Ride Rockit

🎟 Yes 📏 51"-79" 📷 Yes ⊘ 2 minutes ⏳ 45 to 90 minutes 🔒 Yes

Hollywood Rip Ride Rockit is a unique coaster that dominates the skyline from the moment you step foot inside the park.

Once on-board, prepare to be held in by just a lap bar-style restraint as you start your vertical climb to the top.

On this ride, you get to choose from a pre-selected number of songs to play during your ride. Your choice of music will pump into your ears through individual seat speakers as your adrenaline races.

Think of this as *Rock 'n' Rollercoaster* from Walt Disney World but with more music choices, without the loops and a bigger drops.

Straight after the first drop, you enter a unique 'almost-a-loop' that is really fun; you do a loop but stay upright all the way round - a really unique experience.

Once the experience is over, in addition to on-ride photos, you can even purchase a music video of your ride filmed using on-board cameras and including your choice of song as the soundtrack!

A Single Rider line is available at this attraction.

Top Tip: Don't trust the Single Rider wait time that posted at the attraction entrance. We have often waited less than half of the official posted Single Rider wait.

To help you estimate, enter the Single Rider line - from the bottom of the stairs to being on the train is usually about 30 minutes.

Top Tip 2: As well as the songs displayed on the screen, there are many secret bonus songs that you can choose from.

To access them, after closing your restraint, you will need to push and hold the ride logo on the screen for about 10 seconds. When you let go a number pad appears; type in a three-digit number for load the song.

A full list of the songs is available online with a quick search.

Top Tip 3: The "Pocket RockIt Rollercoaster Setlist" iPhone app, available on the Apple App Store, also lists the full song list including hidden songs. The app costs $0.99.

TRANSFORMERS: The Ride-3D

🎟 Yes	📏 40"	📷 No	⊙ 4 minutes	⏳ 90 to 150 minutes	🔒 No

TRANSFORMERS is a 3D screen-based moving dark ride, similar to *The Amazing Adventures of Spider-Man* at *Universal's Islands of Adventure*.

The storyline follows the Autobots trying to get the Allspark.

Your ride vehicle moves from set to set, acting as a moving simulator immersing you in the action.

TRANSFORMERS: The Ride will be doubly impressive to fans of the movie franchise, though those who have not seen them are still likely to enjoy the experience.

Out only issue with the ride is its similarity to the *Spider-Man* attraction in the theme park next door. Considering *Spider-Man* is over 15 years old, it feels like almost no technological or storytelling progress has been made since then. Plus, we have a personal penchant for the *Spider-Man* characters.

This ride often has one of the longest queues in the park, so try to get here early in the day or towards the end, when crowds are at their lightest.

A Single Rider line is also available - we have found that it typically reduces you wait to half or less than the regular standby line.

An engineering masterpiece: Ever wondered how such a long ride is packed into such a small building?

Universal's engineers came up with an ingenious way to reduce the ride's overall footprint: during the ride, while you are watching a scene on one of the giant screens, you are taken in an elevator up one floor that houses another level of track.

Here the ride continues its course and you later come back down to the first floor via another elevator while you watch another giant screen – this is all done seamlessly and really is an incredible feat.

DINING

Universal Studios' Classic Monster Cafe – Quick Service. Accepts Universal Dining Plan. Serves chicken, lasagne, cheeseburgers, pizza and other fast-food style meals. Entrées are priced at $7.50 to $11.50.

New York

This area of the park is themed around the big apple. This was formerly the area of an attraction called TWISTER, but that has now closed and is being replaced by a Jimmy Fallon attraction in 2017.

Attractions

Revenge of the Mummy

Yes | 48" | Yes | 4 minutes | 20 to 60 minutes | Yes

An unique rollercoaster featuring fire, smoke, forward and backwards motion, and more.

The whole ride is fantastic and is one of the most fun coasters we have been on, starting off as a slow moving dark ride and then turning into a traditional coaster.

Although the ride does not go upside down, and is not exactly the fastest attraction in Orlando, it does tell its story very well and really immerses you in the atmosphere. It is a great thrill, with plot twists throughout.

The queue line is also really detailed and contains several interactive elements.

For example, there is a scarab beetle that you can press while watching other guests via a screen. If you press the beetle, the guests will feel a quick blast of air from underneath them, guaranteed to give them a fright.

But beware where you put your hands while waiting in line, as the treasure you see around you may not be all you think it is, and you might just be in for a surprise or two.

A Single Rider queue line is available. We recommend first-timers see the regular standby line once before using the Single Rider queue.

Fun Fact: *Revenge of the Mummy* replaced *Kongfrontation* (a ride based on King Kong), that was previously housed in the same building; a statue of the great ape has been left behind as a tribute in the treasure room. See if you can spot it!

The Blues Brothers Show

See Jake and Elwood, the Blues Brothers, take to the stage in this show.

Unlike other shows where you sit in a show-style amphitheater, *The Blues Brothers*

Show takes place on a small stage in a street with more of a street-performer feel to it. Crowds are not very big and most people just walk in and out during the show.

Rock climbing

Next to *Revenge of the Mummy*, there is a small alleyway that has a 50-foot tall rock-climbing wall.

Climb it and once you reach the top, ring the bell to claim victory!

Race Through New York Starring Jimmy Fallon

Of all the attractions opening in 2017, this is the one that we know the least about as Universal has still not released any details.

It has been confirmed that this will be a 3D experience, but that is all we know at the moment - it could be a simulator, or it could be a theatre-style show.

Universal's press release says:
"The adventure will begin as guests step right into Studio 6B, where Jimmy will challenge them and their fellow audience members to a white-knuckle race."

"Guests will twist, turn and laugh as they speed through the streets –

and skies – of The Big Apple – encountering everything from iconic landmarks to the deepest subway tunnels – and anything else that comes to Jimmy's mind."

DINING

Finnegan's Bar and Grill – Table Service. Accepts Universal Dining Plan. Serves salads, sandwiches, fish and chips, chicken, corned beef, sirloin steak and more. Entrées are priced at $10 to $22. This is our favorite place to eat in this park outside of Diagon Alley.
Louie's Italian Restaurant – Quick Service. Accepts Universal Dining Plan. Serves spaghetti and meatballs, pizza slices, whole pizza pies and fettuccine alfredo. Entrées are priced at $6 to $14. Whole pizza pies are priced between $29 and $36.

World Expo

World Expo is home to both a MEN IN BLACK attraction, as well as a Simpsons area. Fear Factor: LIVE is the live show in this area.

Attractions

MEN IN BLACK: Alien Attack

 Yes | 42" Yes | 5 minutes | Less than 45 minutes | Yes

At *Men In Black*, your mission is to protect the city and defeat the attacking aliens. You are sent in teams and, using handheld laser guns, compete against another team of riders to defeat the aliens and get a high-score.

This ride is a fun, family-friendly experience that we highly recommend. A Single Rider line is available.

Top Tip: Hold down the trigger throughout the ride. You get points for doing this, regardless

of whether you hit any targets or not.

For major points, find and shoot Frank the Pug who is hidden on the ride; Frank is in the newspaper stand on the right side of the second room.

Fear Factor Live

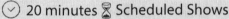 Yes | None No | 20 minutes | Scheduled Shows | No

Get ready to watch theme park guests face their fears live on stage as they compete against each other in *Fear Factor Live*.

Alternatively, why not apply and be one of those guests? To participate in the show,

you will want to be near the entrance 60 to 90 minutes before show time. Guests must be over 18, have photo ID on them and be in good physical condition to participate.

Volunteers are also chosen to play minor

roles during the show.

This show is starting to show its age, in our opinion, and we expect it to be replaced in the coming years, but for the moment it's a fun distraction - especially if you have never seen it before.

The Simpsons Ride

Yes | 40" | No | 6 minutes | 20 to 40 minutes | No

The Simpsons Ride brings the famous yellow Springfield family to life in a fun-filled rollercoaster simulator-style ride in front of an enormous screen.

Your adventure is filled with gags throughout and is a fun family experience. Simpsons fans will love this ride!

Fun fact: During the pre-show video, look out for the DeLorean car and Doc Brown from Back to the Future. This is a tribute to the *Back to the Future* attraction that previously occupied the same building.

Kang and Kodos' Twirl 'N' Hurl

This is a fairly standard fairground-style spinning ride, like Disney's Dumbo attraction. Here, you sit in flying saucers and spin around. A lever allows you to control the height of your saucer.

Around the attraction there are pictures of Simpsons characters; when you fly past them, they speak.

There is no Express Pass for this attraction but wait times are generally 10 minutes or less, except during peak days.

The Springfield Area: There are many photo opps here, including a giant Lard Lad donuts, Chief Wiggum by his police car, a statue of Jebediah Springfield, Duff Man flexing his muscles and more. Characters often meet in this area, and there are carnival games you can pay to play.

DINING

Fast Food Boulevard – Quick Service. Accepts Universal Dining Plan. From the outside, it looks like several separate Simpsons buildings. Inside, it is actually one area.
• **Moe's Tavern** sells Buzz Cola, Flaming Moes and Duff Beer ($3 to $8)
• **Lisa's Teahouse of Horror** sells salads and wraps ($6 to $10)
• **Luigi's** sells personal-sized pizzas ($7 to $8)
• **The Frying Dutchman** sells fish ($4 to $14)
• **Cletus' Chicken Shack** sells fried chicken and chicken sandwiches ($8 to $11)
• **Krusty Burger** sells burgers and hot dogs ($8 to $13)

Duff Brewery – Bar with snacks. Drinks are $3-$8, a hot dog is $8 and chips are $2.80.
Bumblebee Man's Tacos – Quick Service. Drinks are $3 to $6.50, tacos are $7 to $9.

Hollywood

Attractions

Universal's Horror Make Up Show

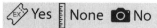 Yes | None No ⊘ 25 minutes ⧗ Scheduled Shows 🔒 No

Go behind the scenes and see how gory and horror effects are created for Hollywood movies in this fun and educational show that is sure to have you in stitches.

The script is very well thought out, with laugh after laugh, and some fun audience interaction too. This is one show we highly recommend you visit! The theatre is relatively small so be sure to arrive early.

If you want to be part of the show, the hosts tend to choose young women in the middle section of the theatre. They also tend to go for someone who they think will speak no English, for comedic effect.

Terminator 2: 3-D

Yes | None 🔘 No ⊘ 25 minutes ⧗ Less than 15 minutes 🔒 No

Terminator 2: 3-D is an incredible mix of live-action, 3D and in-theatre special effects. This show is unlike any theme park show we have ever seen and is a really enjoyable watch.

The 3D is incredibly well accomplished and merges seamlessly with the live actors; sometimes it is difficult to figure out what is on screen and what is actually in front of you.

If you do not enjoy loud noises, then Terminator 2 is most definitely not for you, but it would be a shame to miss out on such an incredible show. The show runs about every 20 to 45 minutes.

DINING

Mel's Drive In – Quick Service. Serves cheeseburgers and root beer floats. Accepts Universal Dining Plan. Entrées are priced at $8 to $10.50.
Beverly Hills Boulangerie – Quick Service. Accepts Universal Dining Plan. Serves sandwiches, pastries, cakes, soups and salads. Entrées are priced at $7 to $12.

San Francisco

This area of the park has changed immensely over the years, especially since the closure of the Jaws ride to make way for The Wizarding World of Harry Potter: Diagon Alley a few years ago.

Now, San Francisco is once again going through a major redevelopment. "Disaster!" and "Beetlejuice's Graveyard Revue" both closed in 2015. This area is being redeveloped to make way for a brand new ride – Fast & Furious: Supercharged – opening in 2017.

Attractions
Fast & Furious: Supercharged

In 2018, the San Francisco area of the park will welcome a new attraction.

Universal says that the *Fast & Furious* attraction will "fuse everything you love about the films with an original storyline and incredible ride technology. You'll get to check out some of the high-speed, supercharged cars you've seen on the big screen. You'll be immersed in the underground racing world made famous in the films and explore the headquarters of Toretto and his team. Then, you'll board specially-designed vehicles for an adrenaline-pumping ride with your favorite stars from the films."

Expect big screens simulating a race and simulator-style action.

DINING

Richter's Burger Co. – Quick Service. Accepts Universal Dining Plan. Serves cheeseburgers, salads, and chicken sandwiches. Entrées are priced at $8 to $10.50.
Lombard's Seafood Grille – Table Service. Accepts Universal Dining Plan. Serves salads, sandwiches, catch of the day, sirloin steak, stir-fry and more. Entrées are priced at $9 to $22.
San Francisco Pastry Company – Sandwiches and Pastries. Accepts Universal Dining Plan. Entrées are priced at $3 to $9.50.

Woody Woodpecker's Kid Zone

This is the area of the park dedicated to the smaller members of the family. As you will see, Universal isn't just for adrenaline junkies.

Attractions

E.T. Adventure

Yes | 34" | No | 5 minutes | Less than 20 minutes | No

A cute, if ageing, ride where you sit on bicycles, like in the E.T. movie, and soar through the sky while trying to keep E.T. safe.

It is a fun little ride with a fairly high capacity and one of the few *Universal Studios Florida* classics that remains from the park's opening day.

The ride system allows you to 'cycle through the air' and makes for a truly immersive experience. If you do not like heights, avoid this attraction.

A Day in the Park with Barney

Yes | None
No | 15 minutes
Scheduled Shows
No

Join Barney and his friends for a fun-filled show where little ones can even sing along. After the show, there is a play area, and you can meet Barney.

Curious George Goes to Town

A water play area. Be sure to bring a change of clothes for the little ones.

Fievel's Playland

A play area for the little ones to let off some steam. There is quite a lot of water here, including a dinghy slide, so be sure to bring a change of clothes.

Animal Actors on Location

🎟 Yes | None 📷 No | ⊙ 20 minutes ⧗ Scheduled Times | 🔒 No

A behind the scenes look at how animals are taught to act in films – there is even some audience participation.

Animal fans will enjoy it but in our opinion, the show is lacklustre with a big reliance on video clips and a lack of flow. It is a shame to see this show, especially when compared to a similar show at *Disney's Animal Kingdom* that only features birds – Disney's show has humor, a great storyline and a real wow factor. This one just doesn't. We would advise you to give this a miss unless you are a big animal fan.

Woody Woodpecker's Nuthouse Coaster

🎟 Yes | 36" 📷 No | ⊙ 44 seconds ⧗ Less than 30 minutes | 🔒 No

Think of *Woody Woodpecker's Nuthouse Coaster* as a kid's first coaster – a way to get them introduced into the world of coasters before trying something a bit more intense.

The ride is great fun for the little ones or just for those not wanting to jump on the likes of *The Incredible Hulk Coaster* just yet.

It is a short ride, but should be more than enough to please young thrill seekers.

DINING

There are no dining locations in this area of the park.

The Wizarding World of Harry Potter: Diagon Alley

The Wizarding World of Harry Potter is one of the best known areas at Universal, and it is split between the two theme parks. Hogsmeade is in Islands of Adventure, and Diagon Alley is in Universal Studios Florida.

Diagon Alley cannot be seen by Muggles (non-Wizards), so it is hidden behind a recreation of London's Waterfront.

On the waterfront are façades of London landmarks. As well as the façades, visitors see the Statue of Eros, and the Knight Bus.

This Knight Bus features an interactive shrunken head experience as seen in the Prisoner of Azkaban film.

Visitors enter Diagon Alley through Leicester Square station and transition into the Wizarding World via brick walls and the help of some sound effects.

Shops

• **Quality Quidditch Supplies** – Sells apparel, hats and pendants, brooms, Golden Snitches, and Quaffles.

• **Weasleys' Wizard Weezes** – Sells prank items, toys, novelty items and magic tricks, such as Extendable Ears and Decoy Detonators.

• **Madam Malkin's** – Find Hogwarts school uniforms, with ties, robes, scarves, and more. Also sells jewelry themed to the four school houses.

• **Ollivander's** (show and shop) – See a wand pick a wizard, and buy your own.

• **Wiseacre's Wizarding Equipment** – From hourglasses to compasses, and telescopes to binoculars.

• **Wands by Gregorovitch** – The legendary wand shop.

• **Shutterbuttons** – Get a personalized "moving picture" just like the Harry Potter newspapers for $49.95. Up to 4 people can partake in the experience. You are supplied with robes, but you must bring your own wand.

Dining

Fans of the boy wizard will definitely not go hungry in Diagon Alley:

• **Leaky Cauldron** – Quick Service. Accepts Universal Dining Plan. Serves traditional English fare such as Banger's and Mash, Toad in the Hole, Fish and Chips and more. Entrées are $9 to $20.

• **Florean Fortescue's Ice Cream** – Quick Service. Serves ice cream and other treats, as well as breakfast items and pastries in the morning. Does not accept the Universal Dining Plan. Flavors include: Earl Grey and Lavender, Clotted Cream, Orange Marmalade, Butterbeer, and others. Ice creams are $5 to $13. We highly recommend the Butterbeer ice cream – its delicious.

Diagon Alley also includes shopfront façades that make for great photo ops, such as the offices of the Daily Prophet, Broomstix, Flourish and Blotts, etc.

Knockturn Alley

Running alongside Diagon Alley, is the darker "Knockturn Alley", described as a "gloomy back street" by Universal. The shops and store fronts here are filled with items related to Dark Magic.

The flagship store here is Borgin and Burkes, which sells dark items such as Death Eater masks, skulls and other sinister objects. Make sure to check out the vanishing cabinet.

This area is covered so it is continually dark and creates a nighttime atmosphere. Expect it to be popular during Orlando's frequent rain showers.

Be sure to look out for the animated "Wanted" posters of the Death Eaters. The window with the tarantulas on it might give you a bit more than you bargained for as well, if you get too close.

There are also many interactive wand experiences available in this area (more on these later). Two other streets in Diagon Alley have themed shop fronts and interactive wand touches – Horizont Alley and Carkitt Market.

Attractions

Harry Potter and the Escape from Gringotts

🎟 No | 📏 42" | 📷 Yes | ⏱ 5 minutes | ⏳ 30 to 60 minutes | 🔒 Yes

Outside Gringotts bank, marvel at the fire-breathing dragon on the roof. Then, once inside, prepare for the experience of a lifetime.

The queue line begins by going past animatronic Goblins hard at work in the grand marble lobby, followed by wizard vaults and a security area (where you have your photo taken). You even board a huge elevator while waiting.

Just like *Harry Potter and the Forbidden Journey* in *Islands of Adventure*, this attraction's queue line is as much of an experience as the ride itself. The storyline begins to unfold as you see signs of Harry, Ron and Hermione discussing their plans.

The ride itself is a "multidimensional" rollercoaster-type attraction. It mixes a real world elements with footage on huge screens, much like *Forbidden Journey*.

There are drops and turns (but no loops or inversions) in the layout, and it is more a 3D-style ride than a rollercoaster - more *Transformers* than *The Incredible Hulk*. The ride features 4K-high definition technology as well as 3D screens, with glasses being worn by riders.

A Single Rider line is available, but it skips all the queue line scenes and leads directly to the loading area. Remember that the queue is a significant part of the experience here. However, if all you want is the ride itself, the Single Rider line can save you a significant amount of time.

Storyline – Spoiler Alert: The ride is inspired by the final film "Harry Potter and the Deathly Hallows – Part 2," and a pivotal scene where Harry, Ron and Hermione break into Gringotts bank to steal a powerful Horcrux to help them defeat Lord Voldemort. On *Harry Potter and the Escape from Gringotts*, you will encounter the trio during this quest – but expect to meet some dangerous creatures and malicious villains as well! During the ride you will come face to face with Bellatrix Lestrange, security trolls, fire breathing dragons and even Voldemort himself.

Kings Cross Station and the Hogwarts Express

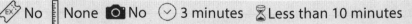
No None No 5 minutes 15 to 60 minutes No

At *Kings Cross Station*, guests can break through the wall onto Platform 9 ¾, and catch the *Hogwarts Express.* This real train ride will transport you through the countryside to *Hogsmeade Station* (located at *Universal's Islands of Adventure*).

The journey lasts several minutes and, as you look out of train windows, you will see stories unfold – all on a full-sized train, with compartments to sit in just like Harry and his pals did in the movies.

During the journey you may see Hagrid on his motorcycle, the English countryside, Buckbeak the Hippogriff, the purple Knightbus, the Weasley twins on brooms, and even some Dementors. There are many more surprises in store, of course. Each of the *Hogwarts Express* trains seats 200 passengers, and trips in both directions are different.

Once you hop off the train at *Hogsmeade* you will be able to explore the area and the Harry Potter

themed attractions, including the incredible *Harry Potter and the Forbidden Journey* ride.

Important: In order to experience the *Hogwarts Express,* you must have a Park-to-Park ticket as you will physically move between theme parks. A Single-Park ticket does not allow you to experience this ride – guests with this ticket can experience each of the theme parks' Wizarding Worlds on separate days, but they cannot travel on the *Hogwarts Express.*

Ollivanders

No None No 3 minutes Less than 10 minutes No

Technically, this is a pre-show to a shop. You enter *Ollivanders* in groups of 25 people. One person is chosen by the wand-master to find the right wand for

them. When the right one is found, they are given the opportunity to buy it in the shop next door. This is a fantastic experience that we highly recommend

you visit. It is suitable for people of all ages. The queue lines at this *Ollivanders* move much more quickly than the one in *Islands of Adventure*.

Interactive Wand Experiences

An interactive wand experience is available at the Wizarding World, both at Diagon Alley and Hogsmeade.

In order to participate, guests must purchase an interactive wand from the Wizarding World's shops. These are priced at $48; $8 more than the non-interactive wands.

Once you have purchased a wand, look for one of the 25+ bronze medallions embedded in the streets that mark locations you can cast spells. You also get a map of the locations included with each wand purchase.

Once standing on a medallion, perform the correct spell: draw the shape of the spell in the air with your wand and say the spell's name. Then, watch the magic happen.

This is a fun bit of extra entertainment, and wands can be reused on future visits.

Diagon Alley Live Entertainment

Inside the Carkitt Market area, two shows are performed daily:

The first show brings to life two fables from The Tales of Beedle the Bard – *The Fountain of Fair Fortune* and The Tale of the Three Brothers. This trunk show uses scenic pieces, props and puppetry designed by award-winning designer Michael Curry.

The second show features a musical performance by The Singing Sorceress: Celestina Warbeck and the Banshees. With a whole lot of soul, this swinging show features songs including *A Cauldron Full Of Hot, Strong Love*, and *You Stole My Cauldron But You Can't Have My Heart*.

As well as the live stage shows, the area hosts many other interactive experiences.

Just outside Diagon Alley, you will find the *Knight Bus* and its two permanent occupants: a shrunken head and the Knight Bus Conductor, who will be more than happy to chat, joke around and take photos with you.

Plus, at *Gringotts Money Exchange* you can exchange Muggle currency for Wizarding Bank Notes, which can be used throughout both Universal theme parks to purchase snacks and in stores.

Stores in the Wizarding World accept regular US dollars too, but these bank notes can make for a cool souvenir.

Early Entry

Staying on-site at a Universal hotel entitles you to early admission into the WWOHP one hour before the general public. This also applies to off-site hotels booked as part of a Universal vacation package online or through an authorized reseller – check this is included in your package. Either *Diagon Alley* or *Hogsmeade* will be open. This changes regularly; check Universal's website to find out which one.

If you do not have early admission, be at the park entrance in advance; guests are often allowed in up to 30 minutes before the opening time.

Drinks and Character Meets

To maintain the integrity of the Potter areas, J.K. Rowling (author of *Harry Potter*) specified that no branded drinks be sold in both Wizarding Worlds – so, you will not find Coca Cola or other branded products here.

You will only find Harry Potter drinks such as Butterbeer, water and some fruit squashes. You are, of course, free to buy drinks elsewhere in the park, and bring it into the Wizarding World.

J.K. Rowling also prohibited character meets. So, you cannot meet Harry, Hermione, Hagrid, Draco, Ron or other characters from the films in the Wizarding World. The exception is the Knight Bus driver.

Crowd Control Measures and The Return Ticket System

J. K. Rowling specifically requested that the buildings in the Wizarding World be made in real size. As such, the Wizarding World is small and accommodates a small number of people.

During periods of peak attendance at the park, Universal Orlando may implement crowd control measures. There are two measures that may be used: a stand-by line to enter the Wizarding Worlds, and a return ticket system. It is not possible to know in advance if these systems will be used – if you are visiting around a major holiday, though, there is a chance.

When the stand-by queue line system is operating, you simply wait in a queue line to get into either Diagon Alley or Hogsmeade, as you would for a ride.

With the return ticket system, you go to a kiosk, select the number of people in your party, choose a return time, and receive a ticket to come back and enter the Wizarding World at the designated time. This works similarly to FastPass+ at Walt Disney World.

If both systems are in use, we recommend getting a return ticket. This way you can use your time to ride attractions elsewhere in the park, and return later. Express Passes do not allow you to bypass this system.

On days when crowd control measures are in place, expect very high wait times for all attractions within the land. This means 90 to 120 minutes for the headline attractions, and 60 minutes for everything else.

The system is only in operation when the lands are full. So, you may find that during certain hours you need a return ticket, but not during others. These measures are also independent between the two parks, so they may in operation at one Wizarding World area but not the other.

Both train stations are located outside of the areas subject to crowd controls. You may ride these without needing a return time and simply stand in the standard waiting line.

Since the opening of Diagon Alley in Summer 2014, crowds are now more evenly spread across both parts of the WWOHP. Therefore, we expect the use of this system to be limited to the very busiest of days only.

Universal Studios Florida Park Entertainment

Universal Studios Florida is home to live entertainment throughout the day. Character meet and greets can be found throughout the park, there is a daily parade and a nighttime spectacular rounds out the fun.

Universal's Superstar Parade

Expect to see the Minions and Gru from *Despicable Me*, Sponge Bob Squarepants and Dora the Explorer, among other characters in the daily *Universal Superstar Parade*.

This parade is great fun for character fans. Both the floats and the characters are great to see, and the upbeat music adds to the fun.

The parade route starts by *Universal's Horror Make Up Show*, moves towards the lagoon, past *TRANSFORMERS*, round the front of *Revenge of the Mummy*, down past the *Universal Stage* and *Despicable Me* and back along *Hollywood Boulevard* ending next to *Universal's Horror Make Up Show* where it started.

One of the best things about *Universal's Superstar Parade* is that it is much less crowded than the parades at Disney's theme parks.

Many people simply do not know it exists; others just go to Universal for the thrill rides.

Having said this, although the parade is enjoyable, it is not up to the standards of a Disney parade. The parade is performed once each day; the time will be printed on your park map.

Top Tip: Twice per day, before the parade starts, there are dance parties hosted by Mel's Drive-In. During the dance parties, floats and characters from the parade come out to meet and greet, dance and sign autographs.

Universal's Cinematic Spectacular: 100 Years of Movie Memories

Universal Orlando bids you goodnight with its "Cinematic Spectacular", a nostalgic viewing of highlights from Universal movies of the last 100 years.

The show takes place every evening on the lagoon in the middle of the park and features water screens, a great soundtrack, fountains and fireworks.

The show is thematically split up into categories such as comedy and horror, with clips from famous films projected onto water curtains.

The 18-minute nighttime show is perhaps more relevant to adults than children due to the age of some clips. This is also more of a projection show than a fireworks show, with pyrotechnics being few and far between.

If you want a front row view, then usually turning up 30 minutes before the show's scheduled start time will easily guarantee you a good spot. If you do not fancy waiting that long, simply turn up a few minutes before show time.

There should never be too many people in front of you, as there is such a large viewing area.

This is not a Disney or even SeaWorld-quality show in our opinion, and if you have high expectations you will be disappointed. Nevertheless, it is worth a viewing but once you have watched it once, we doubt you will stick around for it on other days.

Dining Experience:
There is a Cinematic Spectacular Dining Experience option at Lombard's Seafood Grille that gives you reserved seating for the show. However, even on peak summer days, we never found the area around the lagoon crowded to the point that we would consider this necessary. If you want a good view with a meal included, though, it may be worth a look.

Reservations for the Dining Experience should be made at least 24 hours in advance. Prices are $44.99 for adults and $12.99 for children and include an appetizer, entrée,

dessert and one non-alcoholic beverage, as well as VIP viewing of the nighttime spectacular.

VIP viewing:
Alternatively for another view, there is a reserved VIP area in the Simpsons Springfield area for the cinematic spectacular. Seating here is priced at $15 and is on offer 45 minutes before the show begins.

The price of the VIP area includes gratuity, one cupcake and one non-alcoholic beverage (excluding Flaming Moes); the effective cost of the seating is about $8. If it is busy, and you fancy a dessert, this could be a good option for you.

Our favourite view of the show, without an up-charge, is from the area just outside TRANSFORMERS. Here, you get the best overall view of the show with the screens face-on and the fireworks launched in your line of sight.

Universal's Islands of Adventure

Universal's Islands of Adventure opened in 1999 with many famed attractions such as *The Incredible Hulk Coaster* and *The Amazing Adventures of Spider-Man*, that instantly put it on the world theme park map.

The true revolution for the park, however, came with the opening of *The Wizarding World of Harry Potter: Hogsmeade* in 2010.

Expansion and innovation in the park have not stopped since the *Wizarding World* was unveiled. In this theme park you will not find 'lands' but 'islands'. Together these islands make up *Universal's Islands of Adventure*.

The park hosted 8.8 million guests in 2015.

Live Entertainment at the Park:
Unlike *Universal Studios Florida* next door, here there are no daily fireworks shows or parades.

There are, however, character appearances throughout the various lands, in particular in *Seuss Landing* and *Marvel Superhero Island*. There are no Harry Potter characters in *Hogsmeade*, except for the Hogwarts Express Conductor.

Port of Entry

Perhaps the most beautiful entrance to a theme park in America, Port of Entry transports you to a different time and place.

There are no attractions in this area of the park. Instead, it acts as an entranceway to the Islands of Adventure themselves.

You will find many shops and a few places to eat in this area.

To the right of the welcome arch at Port of Entry, you will find **Guest Services**. Here, you can get help with disability assistance, dining reservations, as well as questions, positive feedback and complaints. **Lost and Found** is also located here.

Lockers, a phone card vending machine and a **payphone** are all located to the left of the archway.

Strollers and **wheelchair rentals** can also be found here. **First Aid** is located inside the Open Arms Hotel building to the right of the entrance archway. There is another First Aid station in *The Lost Continent* by the bazaar.

Fun fact: At the wheelchair and stroller rental place look out for a sign listing the prices of rentals along with several gag items, which have already been "rented out" including a gondola, an aero boat and a rocket car.

DINING

Confisco Grille and Backwater Bar – Table Service. Accepts Universal Dining Plan. Serves wood-oven pizzas, sandwiches, pasta and fajitas. Entrées are priced at $9 to $22. The Backwater Bar has a happy hour daily from 4:00pm to 7:00pm (subject to change).
Croissant Moon Bakery – Quick Service. Accepts Universal Dining Plan. Serves continental breakfasts, sandwiches, paninis, cakes and branded coffee. Entrées are priced between $2.50 and $10. Note: This location is not listed on the map – it is on the right hand side of Port of Entry.
Starbucks – Quick Service. Does not accept the Universal Dining Plan.

Seuss Landing

This area is completely themed around the Dr. Seuss books. To make this land looks completely unique, the theme park designers even made sure there were no straight lines anywhere in this land.

Attractions

One Fish, Two Fish, Red Fish, Blue Fish

EX Yes 48"   📷 No   ⏱ 90 seconds   ⧗ 15 to 45 minutes   🔒 No

A classic spinning ride, like *Dumbo* in the Disney parks. This one, however, packs a bit of a twist. The soundtrack is actually a list of instructions you should follow to stay dry. So when you hear "up, up, up" you will want to steer yourself upwards and be as high as possible to avoid a soaking. This is a fun twist on what can be a bit of an unimaginative type of ride. During colder times the water is turned off. Children under 48 inches (1.22m) must ride with an adult.

Caro-Seuss-el

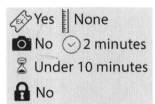

EX Yes ⫯ None
📷 No   ⏱ 2 minutes
⧗ Under 10 minutes
🔒 No

A classic carousel type ride themed to the Seuss series of books.

There is unlikely to be a wait for this ride at any time.

The Cat in the Hat

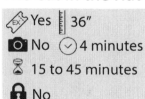

EX Yes ⫯ 36"
📷 No   ⏱ 4 minutes
⧗ 15 to 45 minutes
🔒 No

Spin through the story of The Cat in the Hat. The ride makes more sense if you have read the books or seen the movies, but it is enjoyable for everyone.

If I Ran the Zoo

A play area for children to run around, designed in a maze-like format.

Good for big Dr. Seuss fans, with some in-jokes along the way.

Part of this area is a water play zone to cool down on those hot Floridian days.

The High in the Sky Seuss Trolley Train

| EXP Yes | 40" | 📷 Yes ⊙ | 5 minutes | ⏳ 15 to 45 minutes | 🔒 No |

A cute, slow journey across the rooftops in Seuss Landing. Note how there are no straight lines in this area as you go around the crazy land of Dr. Seuss. The minimum height is 40 inches (1.02m) to ride accompanied, or 48 inches (1.22m) to ride alone.

DINING

Circus McGurks Cafe Stoo-pendous – Quick Service. Accepts Universal Dining Plan. Serves pizza, pasta, salads, cheeseburgers and chicken. Entrées are priced at $7 to $9.

The Lost Continent

Themed to mythological creatures; home to acclaimed restaurant Mythos.

Attractions

Poseidon's Fury

Yes | None | No | 15 minutes | 15 to 45 minutes | No

A combination of a live show and walk-through with cool fire and water effects. Note that this show is standing room only. In our opinion, it is a good watch but not worth more than a 30-minute wait. Return later in the day if queues are long.

The Eighth Voyage of Sindbad Stunt Show

Yes | None | No | 22 minutes | Scheduled Shows | No

An action-packed show filled with special effects. These effects, however, are the problem: the show is just a montage of effects without a storyline.

If you are an action fan watch it; if not, you can skip it.

The Mystic Fountain

A witty, talking, interactive fountain in a courtyard area.

You can ask the fountain questions and have a chat.

The fountain also loves to tell jokes and to get people wet if they come too close!

The fountain only operates at select times of the day.

DINING

Mythos Restaurant – Table Service. Accepts Universal Dining Plan. Serves sandwiches, Shortribs, Asian Salmon and Mahi Mahi. Entrées are $13 to $22. Our favorite in-park restaurant. Only open for lunch.

Fire Eater's Grill – Quick Service. Accepts Universal Dining Plan. Serves hot dogs, chicken fingers and salads. Entrées are $8 to $9. Large portions.

Fun Fact: Stand under the bridge behind Mythos Restaurant to hear a troll.

The Wizarding World of Harry Potter: Hogsmeade

Step into the world of Harry Potter and experience a visit to Hogsmeade. Dine, visit the shops and experience the wild rides. The area is incredibly well themed and Potter fans will see authenticity unlike anywhere else. Throughout this section, you may see The Wizarding World of Harry Potter abbreviated to WWOHP.

The *Hogsmeade* area of the WWOHP existed several years before *Diagon Alley* opened over in *Universal Studios Florida*.

Both the Wizarding World areas are connected by the *Hogwarts Express* – a real train guests can ride.

The attention to detail here is stunning. E.g., in the restrooms, you can hear Moaning Myrtle; and in the rafters of Three Broomsticks, you can see shadows of owls flying about.

Attractions
Dragon Challenge

| Yes | 54" | No | 2 minutes | 60 to 90 minutes | Yes |

See Ron Weasley's car in the queue line, enter Hogwarts and then fly on an incredible inverted coaster.

There are actually two coasters here: the Hungarian Horntail and the Chinese Fireball. These is one queue line for both coasters and then at the end it splits: here you choose which you want to ride.

The queue line goes on for what feels like miles but it does move fairly quickly. If you are claustrophobic, avoid this ride as the queue goes through some very tight caves at one point.

Top Tip: During the outdoor section of the *Dragon Challenge* queue, there is a viewing area. Here you can get some perfect photos of Hogwarts. Alternatively, it is a great place to watch performances on the stage below with no crowds.

Flight of the Hippogriff

🎟 Yes | 36" | 📷 No | ⌄ 1 minute | ⏳ 45 to 60 minutes | 🔒 No

A small rollercoaster where you soar on a Hippogriff and go past Hagrid's hut. Good family fun and a good starter coaster before putting your children on the likes of *The Hulk*.

Hogsmeade Station and the Hogwarts Express

🎟 No | None | 📷 No | ⌄ 5 minutes | ⏳ 15 to 60 minutes | 🔒 No

Guests can catch the *Hogwarts Express*, and be transported through the countryside to *Kings Cross Station* (located at *Universal Studios Florida*).

This is a real moving train that actually transports you between both Universal parks.

The journey lasts several minutes and as you look out of the windows of the train you will see stories unfold – all on a real full-sized train, with compartments to sit in just like Harry and his friends did in the films.

Once you hop off the train at *Kings Cross* you will be by the London waterfront.

From there, you can enter Diagon Alley and explore the Harry Potter themed attractions, including *Harry Potter and the Escape from Gringotts*.

Important: Guests must have a Park-to-Park ticket to ride this attraction. Single Park tickets do not allow entry.

Harry Potter and the Forbidden Journey

No | 48" | Yes | 5 minutes | 30 to 60 minutes | Yes

A truly ground-breaking ride featuring projections, flexible ride vehicles and an incredibly detailed queue.

The opening of this attraction was a turning point in Universal Orlando's history, cementing its spot as one of the world's best theme park resorts.

The queue line of this attraction is an attraction unto itself, as you wind your way through Hogwarts castle watching specially crafted scenes and experiences moments like the famous trio did in the Potter books and movies.

If you do not wish to experience the ride, you can still explore the inside of Hogwarts castle, simply ask one of the team members for the Tour Only entrance.

This allows you to skip the locker queue line and bring cameras to take photos of the incredibly well-themed interior.

At the end of the queue, it is time for an incredible adventure - this is a simulator-style attraction that blurs the lines between physical sets and on-screen projections. Plus, the moment your enchanted bench first takes off is breathtaking.

Expect to encounter dementors, take part in a quidditch match, come face to face with dragons and more.

There is a Single Rider queue line available. This can cut down wait times significantly; waits are usually about 50-75% shorter than the standard wait time in our experience, though this varies.

Warning: We have found that this ride creates an incredible amount of mental strain due to the simulated sensations and the use of the screens in front of you. This means that if you ride it more than once back-to-back, you are likely to feel unwell.

Hidden Secret: When you are in Dumbledore's office hearing his speech, take a look at the books on the wall to the right of him. Once in a while, one of the books may just do something very magical.

Hidden Secret 2: Look at the moving portraits of the four founders of Hogwarts in the queue line; each of them is holding a Horcrux used to defeat Voldemort in the films and books.

Shops

The shops and merchandise here are as much of an experience as the rides. Be sure to step inside to admire the detail.

• **Filch's Emporium of Confiscated Goods** – The exit shop to the *Harry Potter and the Forbidden Journey* attraction. Inside you will find themed apparel, mugs, photo frames and trinkets. It has almost everything a Potter fan could ever want, and even contains a few items themed to dark magic.

• **Honeydukes** – For those with a sweet tooth. You will find love potion sweets, chocolate frogs (with collectable trading cards), and other candy.

• **The Owlery and Dervish & Banges** – The place for Potter wands, Horcrux replicas and even a scaled down model of the Hogwarts Express. Clothing is also sold, as well as stationary and Quidditch items.

• **The Owl Post** – A real post office where letters or postcards can be sent to friends and family – these get a Hogsmeade postmark and a Potter stamp. You will also find stationary on sale here, as well as owl toys.

Restaurants

The restaurants in Hogsmeade are incredibly well-themed and the Quick Service food here is among the best in the park.

We highly recommend you take a look inside the Hog's Head and Three Broomsticks, even if you do not plan on eating there.

• **Hog's Head** – Quick Service. Does not accept the Universal Dining Plan. This pub is located in the same building as the Three Broomsticks. Serves alcoholic beer, a selection of spirits, non-alcoholic Butterbeer and juices. Drinks are priced at $2.50 to $7.

• **Three Broomsticks** – Quick Service. Accepts Universal Dining Plan. Serves breakfast meals. At lunch and dinner, you will find Cornish pasties, fish & chips, Shepard's pie, smoked turkey legs, rotisserie smoked chicken and spareribs. Entrées are priced at $8 to $15.

HOGSMEAD ENTERTAINMENT

Triwizard Spirit Rally
A six-minute dance contest between two competing wizard schools: men versus women. The men's routine involves complex sword-fighting techniques, while the ladies dazzle with their ribbons and acrobatics. It is a nice bit of entertainment, and a great photo opportunity.

Frog Choir
A nine-minute series of songs inspired by the the Harry Potter movies performed by Hogwarts students and their frogs, all done acapella with voices and no instruments. There is an almost beat-box flair to this show and it is a great piece of live entertainment.

Ollivanders
This is very similar to the Ollivanders attraction at Diagon Alley. This version is older, though. There is only a single show room meaning that wait times be up to 45 minutes. The same experience is available at Diagon Alley but with shorter waits.
Note: This is not listed as an attraction on the park map; and there is no wait time sign. The entrance is the railings to the left-hand side of door to Ollivander's.

Jurassic Park

Since the Jurassic Park movie became a classic in 1993, children and adults alike have dreamed of visiting this magical world of dinosaurs. Universal's Islands of Adventure allows you do just that.

There are several photo opportunities located throughout the land including jeeps with dinosaurs next to them. These jeeps are the actual ones that were used in the first movie!

Attractions

Jurassic Park River Adventure

⏚ Yes   📏 42"   📷 Yes   ⏱ 5 minutes   ⏳ 45 to 90 minutes   🔒 No

Step into the world of Jurassic Park on a river boat, glide past huge dinosaurs, and enter through enormous doors just like in the movies. However, this calm river adventure soon changes course.

Watch out for the T-Rex before you come splashing down an 85-foot drop! A Single Rider line is available at this attraction.

Top Tip: You won't stay dry on this ride, but the back row is less wet.

Note: Lockers are not compulsory for this ride, so be prepared to pay $4 for 90 minutes of locker time. There are also giant human-sized dryers priced at around $5 but we have found these to be ineffective.

Camp Jurassic

A play area themed around the Jurassic Park movies. We definitely recommend exploring the area, as the detail is just incredible. What's more, this play areas

isn't only reserved for children. Here, anyone of any age can explore the area and all it has to offer, from the caves to the water jets and the treetop platforms to the

slides.

Fun Fact: Step on the dinosaur footprints on the ground in this area for a roaring sound.

Pteranodon Flyers

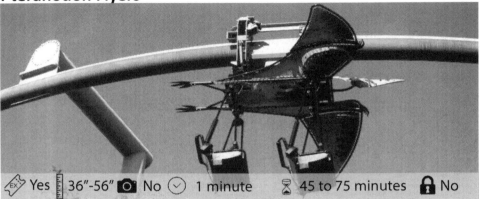

🎟️ Yes | 📏 36"-56" | 📷 No | 🕐 1 minute | ⏳ 45 to 75 minutes | 🔒 No

Soar above Jurassic Park on a winged dinosaur rollercoaster car.

This is the only attraction in the park to have such a restrictive set of requirements.

In order for an adult (or anyone over 56 inches) to ride they must be accompanied by someone under 36 inches tall. This really limits the number of guests who can experience this attraction.

Jurassic Park Discovery Center

An exploration area where you can see model dinosaurs, play dinosaur-themed carnival-style games, learn about DNA sequencing, and witness a dinosaur birth. The main part of the *Discovery Center* is inside the building downstairs.

Top Tip: Exit out the back doors and you will find an outdoor patio area, which is a great place to take long-shot photos of *Islands of Adventure*. You will get great views of *Seuss Landing* and *Marvel Super Hero Island* in particular.

Raptor Encounter

Meet and take photos with a raptor. Be careful! They are unpredictable and loud, but Universal Team Members are around if anything gets out of hand.

The raptors don't walk around the land; you'll find them in their paddocks where they stick their heads through a gap in the fence for photos.

You can take your own photos, but there is also a 'My Universal Photos' photographer present. At the time of writing, appearance times are not posted on the park map but the raptors can usually be met between 11:00am and 4:30pm.

DINING

The Burger Digs – Quick Service. Accepts Universal Dining Plan. Serves burgers, chicken tenders and chicken sandwiches. Entrées are $8 to $10. **Thunder Falls Terrace** – Quick Service. Accepts Universal Dining Plan. Serves cheeseburgers, ribs, smoked turkey legs, wraps, and rotisserie chicken. Entrées are $9 to $16. The portion sizes are large.

Skull Island

Attractions

Skull Island: Reign of Kong

No | 34" | 📷 No | ⊘ 6 minutes | ⏳ 60 to 90 minutes | 🔒 No

The newest attraction at Universal's Islands of Adventure is Skull Island: Reign of Kong.

Step aboard one of the huge 72-seat 4x4 vehicles. Once on board each ride promises to be unique as one of five different drivers takes you on an adventure.

Universal puts it best: "You'll navigate perilous jungles, explore ancient temple structures, and encounter hostile natives – and that's only the beginning.

Throughout the rest of your excursion, you'll brave foreboding caves crawling with prehistoric creatures, fend off unspeakable terrors – and even come face-to-face with the colossal Kong himself."

The animatronics, music and atmosphere created here are second to none and we expect *Reign of Kong* to remain one of the most popular attractions in the park for a while - we anticipate the wait times for *Reign of Kong* will be the highest in the park for the next year or two, or until another attraction takes its place as the newest.

Express Pass access is currently not available.

To minimise your wait times, make this either the first attraction you visit during the day - or the last.

A Single Rider line is available - wait times here are usually about half of the regular queue line.

Top Tip: If you want to see Kong up close, sit on the right had side of the vehicle - each side provides a different and unique experience. The drivers also change up the experience too.

Toon Lagoon

Toon Lagoon is an entire land dedicated to water – with two of the park's water attractions here, as well as water elements everywhere in the area.

Attractions

Dudley Do-Right's Ripsaw Falls

 Yes   44"   📷 Yes ⊙ 7 minutes   ⏳ 45 to 75 minutes   🔒 No

Want a water ride that gets you absolutely soaked? You should give this one a try.

The ride contains a well-themed interior and culminates in

several drops with a final rollercoaster-like splashdown making sure you leave thoroughly drenched. The ride reaches a top speed of 45mph (over 70 km/h), so you get a great thrill!

A Single Rider queue line is available at this attraction.

Optional lockers are available for a fee.

Popeye & Bluto's Bilge-Rat Barges

 Yes   42"

📷 No   ⊙ 6 minutes

⏳ 45 to 90 minutes

🔒 No

Popeye's will make sure you come out drenched from head to toe. This is by far the wettest water

ride at Universal and it is a whole lot of fun along the way. Universal has come up with creative ways to wet you.

Optional lockers are available; the center of the raft has a covered section for some water protection too.

Me Ship, The Olive

This is a kids play area and a great place for a break from the crowds.

For those who like causing chaos, there are free water cannons on the top level of the ship to spray guests on the Popeye water ride below.

DINING

Blondie's – Quick Service. Accepts Universal Dining Plan. Serves sandwiches, made to order subs and hot dogs. Entrées are priced at $9 to $9.50.

Comic Strip Cafe – Quick Service. Accepts Universal Dining Plan. Serves Chinese beef and broccoli, chilidogs, sandwiches, fish & chips, pizza, and spaghetti and meatballs. Entrées are priced at $7.50 to $14.

Marvel Super Hero Island

This island contains two of our favourite attractions in all of Universal Orlando – Spider-Man and The Hulk, as well as fun comic book theming, places to eat and shop, and other attractions. You will often find Marvel characters meeting guests in this area of the park.

Attractions
The Amazing Adventures of Spider-Man

 Yes | 40" Yes ⊘ 5 minutes ⧗ 45 to 75 minutes No

One of the most ground-breaking rides in the world, *The Amazing Adventures of Spider-Man* is a world-class attraction that incorporates projection screens with real world elements like never seen before.

More than a decade after its opening, the attraction has not aged a single bit, as it has been updated with 4K and 3D technology creating higher resolution images. The storyline works as well as it ever has.

The ride still wins awards and is a fun experience swinging around New York City with Spider-Man. It is an absolute must-do a.

This ride operates a Single Rider line, which can usually save you a lot of time.

Doctor Doom's Fearfall

Yes | 52" No ⊘ 45 seconds ⧗ 45 to 60 minutes No

Love drop towers? Then you will adore this ride.

Doctor Doom needs your screams for power; to get them, he shoots you up in the air – and

he definitely gets more than enough power.

This rid itself is one high speed launch up, followed by a free-fall back down (and then

up and down until you stop).

This attraction operates a Single Rider queue line – ask for it at the entrance.

The Incredible Hulk Coaster

🎟 Yes   📏 54"   📷 Yes   ⊘ 2 minutes   ⏳ 30 to 90 minutes   🔒 Yes

Winner of numerous awards, *The Incredible Hulk Coaster* is our favorite rollercoaster in all of Orlando.	It is a truly outstanding thrill with huge loops, an underground section, and non-stop fun from the moment you are launched out of the tunnel until you are back at the station.	There is a Single Rider line at this attraction; just ask the ride attendant at the front to use it – the waits are often short as it is not well signposted.

Storm Force Accelatron

🎟 Yes   📏 48"   📷 No   ⊘ 1 minute   ⏳ Under 10 minutes   🔒 No

A standard teacup style ride themed to Marvel super hero, Storm - but fast! An adult must accompany those under 48 inches (1.22m)

DINING

Captain America Diner – Quick Service. Accepts Universal Dining Plan. Serves cheeseburgers, chicken sandwiches, chicken fingers and salads. Entrées are priced at $8 to $10.50.
Cafe 4 – Quick Service. Accepts Universal Dining Plan. Serves pizza, pasta, sandwiches and salads. Entrées are priced at $6 to $9.

Volcano Bay

2017 sees the arrival Universal Orlando's first on-site water theme park. At the time of writing, Universal has released limited details - here is what we know.

Universal Orlando's third theme park will be a next-generation water park.

What can I expect?
The concept art that has been released is featured on this page and shows us that we can expect a mix of both thrills and relaxation. From fun water slides winding thir way through the park's iconic volcano, to a wave pool for the whole family. Volcano Bay is made up of four incredibly themed areas with Polynesian influences ranging from Easter Island, Hawaii, New Zealand and more.

When will it open?
No exact opening date has been announced at the time of writing but Universal has said it will be open "by June 1, 2017".

Will the park be open all year round?
As this is Universal's first water park, we can only make an educated guess as to how it will work. We expect the park to be open year-round, perhaps with an annual maintenance period of a month or two, or - most likely - slides will go down one at a time throughout the year for maintenance, like at the theme parks.

How much will admission cost?
Volcano Bay will not be included in your regular park admission, and will most likely be an optional extra. We expect a standalone ticket to Volcano Bay to be in the $50 to $60 price range, and possibly as an add-on to a park ticket for $40 or so.

How will it be unique?
Universal says: "We found a way to get rid of long lines. We made it so you don't have to carry your tube. We spread amenities like dining throughout the park, so you don't have to hike up to the front of the parke to eat."

We think Volcano Bay may implement a ride reservation system, but this has not been confirmed.

Park Areas

Krakatau:
At the heart of the park, you'll see the 200-foot-tall volcano called Krakatau. By day, you'll see its majestic waterfalls. And by night, the volcano will illuminate with blazing lava.

Three body slides are found at the rear of the volcano, and each starts off with surprise doors that drop out from beneath you:
• Ko'okiri Body Plunge: A racing, 70-degree drop that will plummet 125-feet through the center of Krakatau. It will be the world's first slide to travel through a pool filled with guests.
• Kala and Ta Nui Serpentine Body Slides: Two intertwining slides where you'll fall freely along 124 twisting feet.
• Punga Racers: A high-speed race through four different enclosed slides featuring manta-shaped mats.
• Secret Attraction: "It'll be like nothing else in the park" but we have no more details.

Wave Village:
Located at the base of Krakatau, Wave Village is a perfect place to soak in the sun and relax on the sandy shores. It includes:
• Waturi Beach: A multi-directional wave pool where you can swim, relax on the sand or indulge in private, one- or two-story cabanas.
• The Reef: An adjacent leisure pool with calmer waters and views of riders on the Ko'okiri Body Plunge.

River Village:
River Village offers several family-friendly attractions and experiences and features:
• Kopiko Wai Winding River: A gentle, winding river that passes through the volcano's hidden caves, featuring spontaneous water effects and a journey through the cave of starlight.
• Tot Tiki Reef: A toddler play area with spraying Maori fountains, slides and a kid-size volcano.
• Runamukka Reef: A three-story water playground inspired by the coral reef with twisting slides, sprinklers and more.
• Honu: An adventurous, multi-passenger raft ride that will soar across a dual wall.
• Ika Moana: A twisting, multi-passenger raft ride that will glide across bubbling geysers.

Rainforest Village:
Features an incredible assortment of attractions for thrill-seekers, including:
• Maku: North America's first "saucer ride", sending multi-passenger rafts speeding around three saucer-shaped curves.
• Puihi: A multi-passenger raft ride that will plunge you into darkness before bursting into a funnel and a zero-gravity drop.
• Ohyah and Ohno Drop Slides: Two twisting, adrenaline-pumping slides that launch you four- or six-feet above the water at the end.
• TeAwa The Fearless River: An action-packed, racing torrent river where you'll have to hang tight in your inner tube amidst roaring, whitewater rapids.
• Taniwha Tubes: Four unique Easter Island-inspired slides with rafts for single or double riders.
• Puka Uli Lagoon: A tranquil pool where you can swim and relax.

CityWalk

Universal's CityWalk is located just outside the theme parks, and within walking distance of all the on-site hotels. There are shops, restaurants, bars, cinemas and clubs.

CityWalk is Universal Orlando's entertainment district, open from 11:00am to 2:00am every day of the year.

CityWalk has been compared to Disney Spring, but since Disney's area had a massive expansion in 2016, it is no longer fair to compare the two. Disney Springs is a heavily themed, shopping mall essentially, with dining locations and a small-town atmosphere.

CityWalk has more of an adult feel to it, particularly at nighttime when there is a heavy focus on the club-like atmosphere. The number of shops and dining locations are also much more limited. It still, however, manages to still keep a fun and friendly atmosphere no matter the time of day.

Like Disney Springs, there is no admission required to enter *CityWalk* - anyone can explore the area for free. Parking, however, is charged before 6:00pm. Parking is at the main Universal parking garages that you park at for the theme parks.

To get details on restaurant and attraction operating hours, recorded information is available by calling (407) 363-8000.

CityWalk has its own Guest Services outpost, which is well signposted and is located next to the restrooms. Also located nearby is **First Aid**.

From *CityWalk* you can catch the complimentary water taxi service to *Sapphire Falls Resort, Royal Pacific Resort, Portofino Bay Hotel,* and *Hard Rock Hotel*. You can also walk to all the on-site hotels from here.

Room keys are not necessary to board the water taxi service most of the day, but these are asked for during the late hours.

Dining

CityWalk is filled with unique dining experiences allowing you to have a taste of Italy, New Orleans, Jamaica and the USA all in one place.

This section helps you choose where to eat on your visit.

Prices for entrées quoted in this section are for adult meals; children's meals are often much cheaper.

Quick Service:

Auntie Anne's Pretzel Rolls – Accepts Universal Dining Plan (snacks). Serves soft pretzels. A pretzel and a drink combo is priced at $6 to $8.

Bread Box Handcrafted Sandwiches – Accepts Universal Dining Plan. Serves sandwiches and salads. Entrées priced at $6 to $8.

Burger King 'Whopper Bar' – Does not accept Universal Dining Plan. Serves burgers, wraps and sandwiches.

Cold Stone Creamery – Accepts Universal Dining Plan (snacks). Serves ice cream at $4.50 to $7.

Cinnabon – Accepts Universal Dining Plan (snacks and beverages). Serves cinnamon rolls and ice cream. Ice creams are $5 to $9.50.

Fusion Bistro Sushi & Sake Bar – Does not accept Universal Dining Plan. Serves sushi and sake, as well as drinks.

Hot Dog Hall of Fame – Accepts Universal Dining Plan. Serves hot dogs. Entrées are $7 to $13.

Menchie's Frozen Yogurt – Does not accept Universal Dining Plan. Serves frozen yogurt priced at $0.59 per ounce (28g).

Moe's Southwest Grill – Does not accept Universal Dining Plan. Serves burritos, tacos, fajitas and other southwest dishes. Entrées are $4 to $8.50.

Panda Express – No Universal Dining Plan. Serves Chinese food.

Starbucks Coffee – Accepts Universal Dining Plan for selected snacks and beverages only. Serves coffees, ice-based drinks, sandwiches and pastries.

Table Service:

Antojitos Authentic Mexican Food – Accepts Universal Dining Plan. Serves Mexican-style food. Entrées are $14 to $29.

Bob Marley – A Tribute to Freedom – Accepts Universal Dining Plan. Serves Jamaican-style dishes. Entrées are $9 to $17.

Bubba Gump Shrimp Co – Does not accept Universal Dining Plan. Serves seafood and other dishes. Entrées are $11 to $27.

The Cowfish Sushi Burger bar – Accepts Universal Dining Plan. Serves burgers and sushi. Entrées are $10 to $27.

Emeril's Restaurant Orlando – Does not accept Universal Dining Plan. Serves Louisiana-style food. Entrées are $11 to $39.

Hard Rock Cafe Orlando – Does not accept Universal Dining Plan. Serves burgers, steaks, ribs and other American-style food. Entrées are $10 to $35. Serves breakfast.

Jimmy Buffet's Margaritaville – Accepts Universal Dining Plan.

Serves Floridian and Caribbean inspired food. Entrées are $11 to $39.

NBC Sports Grill & Brew – Does not accept Universal Dining Plan. Sports-bar style setting with 100 TV screens. Serves salads, and American-style food. Entrées are $10 to $45.

Red Oven Pizza Bakery – Accepts Universal Dining Plan. Serves pizza and salads. Whole pies are $12 to $14. Hands down the best pizza at Universal Orlando.

Pat O' Briens – Accepts Universal Dining Plan. A music venue that serves New Orleans-style dishes. Entrées are priced at $10 to $15.

The Toothsome Chocolate Emporium – Enter this Steampunk chocolate factory with full Table Service meals and mouth-watering desserts. New for Fall 2016.

Vivo Italian Kitchen – Accepts Universal Dining Plan. Serves Italian food. Entrées are $11 to $33.

Making Reservations: To make reservations for Table Service establishments, call (407) 224-3663 or visit opentable.com. Emeril's reservations are made

directly on (407) 224-2424. Hard Rock Café Orlando priority seating can be requested online.

You can combine a meal at select locations with a Party Pass for $21 with tax and tip.

A meal plus mini-golf deal is also available for $25, with tax and gratuity, and is a meal from a select CityWalk location, and 18 holes of mini-golf at the *Hollywood Drive-In* course.

Top Tip 1: Most places have happy hours during the day and evening with discounted drinks and snacks. These vary between locations so ask staff for details.

Top Tip 2: Want free *CityWalk* valet parking? Most restaurants will validate your ticket for a two-hour stay between 11:00am and 2:00pm Monday to Friday. Emeril's will validate your ticket at any time. Tipping the valets is still customary.

Top Tip 3: Ask for the free Hard Rock Café VIBE restaurant tour and get an insight into the memorabilia and décor of the café. Available daily from 2:00pm to 9:00pm, simply ask.

Movie Theater

CityWalk features an AMC Universal Cineplex with 20 screens, including one that shows films in IMAX and IMAX 3D.

Tickets prices vary depending on the time of day and several other factors. A ticket for an adult is priced at $10.00 for shows before 3:55pm and $11.60 from then onwards. Children pay $8.40 all day. "AM" Cinema showings on weekends and holidays before midday are $6.50.

Senior tickets for those aged 60 and over are charged at $8.40 to $10.00. Annual pass holders get $3 off showings after 4:00pm. There are upcharges for non-standard tickets. These are: $4 for a 3D movie, $5 for IMAX and $6 for IMAX-3D.

You can combine a standard movie ticket and a meal at select *CityWalk* restaurants for $21.95 including tax and gratuity.

Mini Golf

Hollywood Drive-In Golf is an adventure golf location with two different courses - one themed to sci-fi (*Invaders from Planet Putt*), the other themed to horror movies (*The Haunting of Ghostly Greens*).

The sounds, special effects, lighting and theming truly immerse you in the miniature world you are in. Pricing is $15 per adult and $13 per child. A single course takes between 35 and 45 minutes to complete, with each being made up of 18 holes.

The entrance is located next to the AMC Cineplex box office.

Discounts for Florida residents, military, seniors, AAA members and Universal annual pass holders are available. The mini-golf location is open from 9:00am to 2:00am daily.

Top Tip: Get your mini-golf tickets at least one day in advance at www.hollywooddriveingolf.com and save up to 13% per ticket.

Blue Man Group

The world famous *Blue Man Group* is the staple nighttime show at Universal. The Blue Men create live music with makeshift instruments in a fun and hilarious musical adventure.

The show lasts 1 hour 45 minutes and does not have an interval. The show schedules change daily with no fixed start times and there are between 1 and 3 shows per day, with shows starting between 3:00pm and 9:00pm.

Ticket prices vary depending on the day of the week. Prices on this page do not include tax and are valid from Sunday to Thursday – add $10 per adult and $5 per child for Friday and Saturday shows.

Higher prices apply daily during peak seasons.

A VIP experience is available for $200 per adult and $150 per child. It includes premier seats to the show, the experience includes a backstage tour loaded with Blue Man Group history, a souvenir program and VIP lanyard, popcorn and soda, a merchandise discount, and an exclusive private meet-and-greet and photo opportunity with a Blue Man after the conclusion of the show.

Tickets can be purchased at the box office or by calling 407-BLUEMAN (407-258-3626) or online at www.blueman.com.

Pre-purchasing tickets can save you up to $10 per ticket. An Annual Passholder discount is available with tickets starting at $60 for adults and $30 for children, plus tax.

Money-Saving Tips: Students with a college ID or an ISIC card can get up to two "rush" day-of tickets for $34 each. AAA members can get a discount by showing their membership card.

Military members can also get a discount; visit your local MWR, ITT, and ITR offices to purchase. Buying in advance online will save you up to $10 per ticket.

	Tier 1	Tier 2	Poncho	Premium
Adult	$70	$85	$95	$105
Child	$30	$37.50	$42.50	447.50

CityWalk Nightlife

As far as bars and nightclubs are concerned, you will find Red Coconut Club, Pat O' Briens, CityWalk's Rising Star, the groove and Fat Tuesday. You will also find live music played at Hard Rock Live Orlando. Lone Palm Airport is also an outdoor bar just across from Jimmy Buffet's.

If you fancy partying the night away, take advantage of the $11.99 *CityWalk* Party Pass (annual Passholders get 20% off up to 4 people). The Party Pass allows you unlimited one-night access to all of the following locations: CityWalk's Rising Star, Jimmy Buffett's Margaritaville, the groove, Pat O'Brien's, Red Coconut Club and Bob Marley – A Tribute to Freedom.

Note: A party pass does not grant you entry during special ticketed events.

Without a Party Pass, the cover charge for a single nightclub is $7 and entertainment usually begins at 9:00pm. Hard Rock Café does not have a cover charge.

Top Tip: If you turn up before 9:00pm, you can avoid most cover charges.

For about $3 more, you can get the *CityWalk* Party Pass + Movie ticket which allows you entry to all the aforementioned locations plus entry into one movie on the same day! This can be purchased at Guest Services.

Multi-day tickets and Flextickets include a free Party Pass that is valid for 14 days from first admission to the parks. So, multi-day ticket holders will not need to spend any extra to enjoy the nightlife.

Blue Man Show ticket holders can also use their ticket stub for free *CityWalk* club access.

CityWalk Shopping

If you fancy shopping, there are plenty of places to visit including: Fossil, Fresh Produce, Quiet Flight Surf Shop, Element, The Island Clothing Store, a large Universal Studios Store (where you can get theme park gear without entering the parks) and Katie's Candy Company.

Finally, if you are in the mood for some ink, visit Hart & Huntington Tattoo Company.

For the Little Ones

It may be hard to imagine Universal Orlando as being a place for small kids when rides such as The Incredible Hulk Coaster and Dr. Doom's Fear Fall dominate the skyline. However, although Universal is by no means anything like Disney's parks a few miles down the road, the theme parks have many areas dedicated to children.

Before leaving for the Universal Orlando Resort, we recommend you measure your child to avoid them getting excited about attractions they cannot ride.

There is nothing more disappointing than being slightly too short for a ride they have waited to do for months; ride operators will not bend the rules, even for half an inch, for everyone's safety. See the minimum height requirements for all attractions later in this section.

Remember that every child has a different comfort zone, and some may well be frightened of an attraction even if they do meet the minimum height requirements. Gently prompting and encouraging them to ride is fine; forcing them is not.

Important: Unlike at the Walt Disney World Resort, baby formula and diapers are not sold at the Universal parks.

Universal Studios Florida

The small members of the family will enjoy seeing Gru and the gang at *Despicable Me: Minion Mayhem* (40"/1.02m minimum) in a 3D simulator ride. *E.T. Adventure* (34"/0.87m minimum) can be a little dark but is a relaxing ride – note that some kids may not enjoy the sensation of flying.

Woody Woodpecker's Nuthouse Coaster (36"/0.92m minimum) is a gentle rollercoaster for starters. The surrounding play areas in *Woody Woodpecker's KidZone* are great fun for kids, such as the *Curious George Goes to Town* play area.

For entertainment, kids are sure to love *A Day in the Park with Barney* - a live interactive stage show featuring the dinosaur himself, and the *Universal Superstar Parade* where they can see all their favorite characters.

The Simpsons Ride (40"/1.02m minimum) also features great characters. Note that this attraction may be frightening due to the huge screen and simulated movements.

Islands of Adventure

Kids will love the *Seuss Landing* area with its play areas, meet and greets, and rides for all ages including the *Caro-Seuss-El; One Fish, Two Fish, Red Fish, Blue Fish* (under 48"/1.22m must ride with an adult); and *The High in the Sky Seuss Trolley Train Ride* (40"/1.02m to ride accompanied by an adult, or 48"/1.22m to

ride alone). In *Toon Lagoon,* you will find several water play areas to splash around in. *Marvel Super Hero Island* also features *Storm Force Accelatron* (an adult must accompany those under 48"/1.22m), this is a themed teacup ride. *Me Ship, The Olive* is a fun play area here too.

The *Jurassic Park Centre* is also a fun, educational, place to learn about dinosaurs.

If the kids can't ride *The Hulk,* try *Pteranodon Flyers* (36"/0.92m minimum), *Flight of the Hippogriff* (36"/0.92m minimum) and *The Amazing Adventures of Spider-Man* (40"/1.02m minimum).

Ride Height Requirements

Many attractions at Universal Orlando have height requirements for guests' safety. We list all rides with height limits in ascending order, and what park they are in.

No Minimum Height:
• Shrek 4-D (USF) - No handheld infants
• Storm Force Accelatron (IOA) - An adult must accompany those under 48" (1.22m)
• One Fish, Two Fish, Red Fish, Blue Fish (IOA) – Children under 48" (1.22m) must ride with an adult

34" (0.87m)
• E.T. Adventure (USF)

36" (0.92m)
• Pteranodon Flyers (IOA) – Guests over 56" must be joined by someone under 36".

• Woody Woodpecker's Nuthouse Coaster (USF)
• Flight of the Hippogriff (IOA)
• The Cat in the Hat (IOA) – 36" to ride with an adult, or 48" alone

40" (1.02m)
• The Amazing Adventures of Spider-Man (IOA)
• Despicable Me: Minion Mayhem
• TRANSFORMERS: The Ride-3D (USF)
• The Simpsons Ride (USF)
• The High in the Sky Seuss Trolley Train Ride (IOA) – 40" to ride with an adult, or 48" alone

42" (1.07m)
• MEN IN BLACK: Alien Attack (USF)
• Popeye & Bluto's Bilge-Rat Barges (IOA)
• Jurassic Park River

Adventure (IOA)
• Harry Potter and the Escape from Gringotts (USF)

44" (1.12m)
• Dudley Do-Right Ripsaw Falls (IOA)

48" (1.22m)
• Revenge of the Mummy (USF)
• Harry Potter and the Forbidden Journey (IOA)

51" (1.29m)
• Hollywood Rip Ride Rockit (USF) – Maximum of 79" (2.00m)

52" (1.32m)
• Doctor Doom's Fearfall (IOA)

54" (1.37m)
• Dragon Challenge (IOA)
• The Incredible Hulk Coaster (IOA)

Services

*Universal Orlando offers a variety of services designed to ease their guests'
days, from photo services to Express Passes, and Single Rider queue lines to
package delivery.*

My Universal Photos

"My Universal Photos"
is a photo collection
system that allows
you to collect all your
in-park photos in one
place.

You can get a "My
Universal Photos"
from any in-park
photographer. Each time
you take a photo, simply
hand the photographer
your card - they will
scan it and your photos
will be collected
together.

Before the end of the
day, visit one of the "My
Universal Photos" stores
where you can choose
the best pictures and
have them printed.

You will need a new
"My Universal Photos"
card for each day of
your vacation, unless
you purchase a Photo
Package. All in-park
photos will be deleted
at the end of the
operating day.

Although superficially
the system seems to be
fairly similar to Disney's
Photopass system,
there are nowhere

near as many in-park
photographers (though
the selection of on-ride
photos is impressive).

Photo Package:
The "My Universal
Photos" Photo Package
is a way to pre-pay for
all your in-park photos.
When you buy the
Photo Package, you will
get two "My Universal
Photos"cards on a
lanyard that you scan
any time you have your
photo taken in the park.

All these photos are
automatically uploaded
to the "My Universal
Photos" website where
you can later download
them at full resolution.

"My Universal Photos"
includes on-ride photos,
character photos and
in-park photographer
photos on the same
account!

To get a Photo Package
either visit the "My
Universal Photos" stores
located at the entrance
to each park – these are
clearly signposted. Or,
after riding an attraction
that has an on-ride
photo, visit the ride's
photo desk to purchase
the Photo Package.

You can use your Photo
Package at the locations
listed on the next page.

Universal Studios Florida:
• On Location (Park Entrance Photos)
• E.T.'s Toy Closet & Photo Spot
• SpongeBob SquarePants Meet and Greet
• MEN IN BLACK Alien Attack
• Harry Potter and the Escape from Gringotts
• Shutterbutton's Photography Studio (with the ShutterButton's package)
• Revenge of the Mummy
• Hollywood Rip Ride Rockit
• Donkey Photo Op (near Shrek 4-D)
• TRANSFORMERS Photo Op
• The Simpsons Photo Op
• Roaming characters where applicable
• Despicable Me Store Photo Op

Universal's Islands of Adventure:
• DeFotos Expedition Photography (Park Entrance Photos)
• Spider-Man Photo Op in Alterniverse Store
• In-Queue Photo Op at The Amazing Adventures of Spider-Man
• The Incredible Hulk Coaster
• Dudley Do-Right's Ripsaw Falls
• Jurassic Park River Adventure
• Raptor Encounter
• T-Rex Automated Photo Capture in Jurassic Park
• Harry Potter and the Forbidden Journey
• The High In The Sky Seuss Trolley Train Ride! In-Queue Photo Op
• Roaming characters where available
• The Grinch Seasonal Photo Op

Pricing:
There are a few different Photo Packages to choose from, depending on how long you visit (prices exclude tax):
• One day – $69.99 online, not sold in-park
• Three consecutive days – $89.99 online, and $99.99 in-park
• Fourteen consecutive days – $139.99 online, not available in-park
• Shutterbutton's Photo Package – $139.99 online

For most visitors, the three-day package offers the best value.

As well as the digital photos via a website, the price of the Photo Package also includes: access to the 'Amazing Pictures' app to view your photos on your iOS or Android smartphone; and discounts on in-park ride photo prints.

The three-day package also includes these additional benefits: 1 free 5x7 or 8x10 print in a folder; 1 free 4x6 print; $5.00 5x7 or $10.00 8x10 prints at participating My Universal Photos locations; and $2.00 4x6 prints at participating locations.

The Shutterbutton's Photo Package includes unlimited Digital Downloads for 3 consecutive days; one 5x7 print; one 4x6 Print, and a Shutterbutton's DVD.

Annual pass holders pay $139.99 plus tax and get unlimited photos for the duration of their pass. In-park this will cost $10 more. This can pay for itself quickly!

Top Tip: You can pre-purchase Photo Packages before you go at https://presale. amazingpictures.com/ UniversalFlorida.aspx. Certain options such as the 1-day and 14-day packages can only be bought online.

Ride Lockers

Many of the rides at Universal do not allow you to take your belongings onto them; loose articles must be placed in free lockers.

How to use the in-park lockers:
• Approach a locker station. These are by the entrance to all rides that require their use;
• Select 'Rent a locker' from the touch screen;
• Put your fingerprint on the reader to be assigned a locker;
• Go to the locker, put your belongings inside and press the green button next to the locker to lock the door. It is very important that you press this button to make sure the locker is actually locked! If you forget to press the green button, the locker will automatically lock 5 seconds after the door is closed.

The lockers are free for a certain period of time. This is always longer than the posted wait time. For example, a 90-minute queue for *The Hulk* would typically allow you 120 or 150 minutes of locker rental time to allow you to queue, experience the ride and collect your belongings.

If you keep your stuff in the lockers longer than the free period, charges apply. The charge is $3 for each additional 30 minutes, up to a maximum daily charge of $20.

Lockers for the water rides are not free - thy are $4 for a set period (the wait time plus a margin), and $3 for each extra 30 minutes, up to a maximum of $20.

Top Tip 1: If your free locker time expires because the queue line took longer than expected, tell a Team Member.
Top Tip 2: If you forget your locker number, a feature on the locker terminals can help you.
Top Tip 3: To avoid paying for a water ride locker, walk to another ride where lockers are free. *Forbidden Journey* often has long rental times, for example.

All-day park locker rentals:
Non-ride lockers are available at the entrance to each park – the cost is $10 per day for a standard locker or $12 for a family size locker. You may access these lockers as many times as you want throughout the day, though their non-central location can be a pain.

Universal's Express Pass

Universal Express Pass allows you to skip the majority of the queue lines in both parks for a fee.

As a stand-alone product, Express Pass access costs between $40 and $150 per person per day. The system is free for

Those staying on-site at the *Hard Rock Hotel, Portofino Bay Hotel* and *Royal Pacific Resort* get Express Pass access for no extra charge.

The Express Pass is a card that allows you to enter a separate attraction queue line that is significantly shorter than the regular queue, and drastically reduces your wait times. For shows, you are allowed entry before guests who do not have an Express Pass – usually 15 minutes before the show is due to begin.

Which rides are not included?

Express Passes are valid on all attractions at both theme parks, with the following exceptions: *Harry Potter and The Forbidden Journey, Ollivander's Wand Shop, Pteranodon Flyers, Skull Island: Reign of Kong, Kang & Kodos' Twirl 'n' Hurl, Hogwarts Express* (both stations) and *Harry Potter and The Escape from Gringotts.*

How do I use it?

At an attraction entrance, show your Express Pass to the Team Member. They will scan it and you will be directed to a separate queue line from non-Express Pass guests.

Typically waits will be 15 minutes or less for rides, even on the busiest days – they will often be much shorter.

As you will be in a different queue line to the main one, Express Pass guests may lose some of the storyline told in the queue. This is particularly evident on

Revenge of the Mummy, TRANSFORMERS and *Men in Black.*

There are four types of Express Pass:

• *Universal Express Pass*: Available for purchase both in the parks and online in advance. It allows one ride per participating attraction.

• *Universal Express Unlimited*: Available for purchase online and in the parks. It allows unlimited rides on each participating attraction.

• *Park-To-Park Ticket + Universal Express Unlimited*: Available for purchase online or over the phone (407-224-7840) and includes a regular park admission ticket for both parks and Universal Express Unlimited access every day. These tickets are available in one-day or multiple day versions. The ticket will expire when all park admission days on the ticket are used or 14 days after first use, whichever is sooner.

• On-site Hotel Universal Express Unlimited Pass: This is a perk for on-site hotel guests from the three most expensive hotels. It is included for each person in the hotel room for every day of their stay, including for all of the check in day and all of their check out day. It allows unlimited rides on each attraction. A photo of each guest will be printed onto this pass.

Each member of your party needs their own Express Pass. If you are not using an On-site Hotel Universal Express Unlimited Pass or a Park-To-Park Ticket + Universal Express Unlimited you will need to purchase a separate Express Pass for each day of your trip.

How to Slash the Price of Express Passes:

We mentioned earlier that guests of select on-site hotels get Unlimited Express Pass access during their stay.

This means that staying at the Hard Rock Hotel, Portofino Bay Hotel or Royal Pacific Resort is the best option if you want the Express Passes for your stay. These are luxury hotel resorts with fantastic amenities, and are located right next door to the theme parks. The queue-cutting privileges are just an extra bonus!

Take a look at the kind of money you can save: One night at the Royal Pacific Resort during the busiest season (Holiday) for two adults is $424 including complimentary Hotel Unlimited Express Passes for your entire stay, including check-in and check-out days.

Buying the same Express Passes separately for these days costs $150 per person, per day. For two days, you would be spending $600 on Express Passes. So, by staying at the Royal Pacific Resort you will save just under $200 and stay at a deluxe hotel.

The price gets even better when more people stay in the same room – one night for 4 people at the Royal Pacific Resort during the holiday season costs $454. In this case, you would save almost $800 total on the cost of Express Passes. Even if you don't need the hotel room, it is cheaper to book one, check-in, get your Express Passes and leave straight away.

If you are a family of five, you can get roll-away beds at the on-site hotels for an additional $25 per night, once again reducing the price per person per day.

These savings aren't exclusive to the Holiday season either. You can get them year-round. Let's look at the Value Season in late January: two adults will pay $244 for a one-night stay at the Royal Pacific Resort. The Express Passes for these dates cost $70 per person, per day. Here you will save $36 total.

This isn't the saving of $200 like during the Holiday season, but remember that you get to stay in a luxury hotel room for this price too! Four adults would pay $294 for one night, saving $266 on Express Passes over two days.

Generally, stays longer than one-night become poorer value as these hotels do have expensive nightly rates. To take full advantage of this secret, you should only stay on-site for one night. Two days is more than enough to see everything on offer with Express Pass access!

Do I need an Express Pass?

In our opinion, during extremely busy periods, getting an Express Pass is almost essential to your visit. It guarantees you will not need to wait hours upon hours in queue lines, especially if you have very limited time.

However, Express Passes are expensive and will often double the cost of your visit.

Having said this, with careful planning and by following our Touring Plans, you should be able to do all the rides you want each day.

If you visit for several days, you can usually do all the attractions at both parks in three full days without an Express Pass, even during the busiest seasons. In this case, an Express Pass is not a necessity but you may wish to consider getting one day

of Express Pass access to begin with, and then repeating attractions at a more leisurely pace on other days without an Express Pass.

If you will be visiting outside of the peak periods of school breaks and public holidays, then chances are that an Express Pass not be as beneficial. Outside of peak periods, you often do not need to wait more than 30 minutes for most attractions.

If you want to do both parks in one day, you'll need Express Passes.

Finally, if you do get an Express Pass, we recommend you get the 'Unlimited' version and not the regular version. You want to be able to ride attractions as many times as you wish, not just once each.

Ultimately, if you cannot afford it, do not buy Express Passes. The money spent on them can feed you all day and buy souvenirs. You will not miss out by not getting an Express Pass if you invest the time to get up early and follow our touring plans – yes, you will queue longer than those who have Express Passes, but you will save hundreds of dollars too.

Top Tip 1: Do not buy Express Passes in advance unless you know the parks will be busy. If you are unsure, wait until you are at the parks to see the wait times; this way you can make an informed decision.

Top Tip 2: If you are buying your Express Park tickets at the parks, don't buy them from the Express Pass kiosk outside the park gates – the queue line here is usually much longer than at the kiosks just inside the park.

Top Tip 3: During certain times of the year, there are post-4:00pm Express Passes sold for $40; these are of more value when the park is open later. You need to ask for these specifically, as they are not advertised.

Top Tip 4: The "Park-To-Park Ticket + Universal Express Unlimited" ticket bundle is cheaper than buying park admission and the Unlimited Express Pass separately.

Top Tip 5: The free Hotel Express Pass only applies during regular park hours. During events where a separate admission ticket is required, such as *Halloween Horror Nights*, you will need to buy an event-specific Express Pass.

Single Rider

One of the best ways to significantly reduce your time waiting in queue lines is to use the Single Rider line instead of the regular queue line.

This is a completely separate queue that is used to fill free spaces on ride vehicles. For example, if a ride vehicle can seat 8 people and a group of 4 turns up, followed by a group of 3, then a Single Rider will fill the empty space on the ride vehicle.

This makes the wait times shorter for everyone in the park as all spaces on ride vehicles are filled. Single Riders typically get on much quicker, and the regular queue line moves marginally quicker as all those single riders aren't in it!

If the parks do get extremely busy, then Single Rider lines can be closed. This happens when the wait in the Single Rider line is the same or greater than the regular line, thereby undermining its purpose.

If the queue line is full and cannot accommodate more guests, it will also be temporarily closed.

If the park is almost empty, then sometimes Single Rider lines do not operate either, as there is no need for them.

Some rides have hidden Single Rider lines that are not advertised - in this case simply ask the first attraction host you see (usually at the entrance to the attraction) if the Single Rider queue line is open. If it is, then they will direct you accordingly.

One prime example of this is *The Incredible Hulk Coaster* that does not advertise its Single Rider line. The *Harry Potter and the Forbidden Journey* Single Rider line can also be easily missed if you do not ask for it.

If you are travelling as a group, you can still use the Single Rider queue line – just be aware that you will ride separately, but you can still meet each other after riding.

Single Rider lines are available on: *The Incredible Hulk, The Amazing Adventures of Spider-Man, Harry Potter and the Forbidden Journey, Jurassic Park River Adventure, Dr. Doom's Fearfall, Dudley Do-Right's Ripsaw Falls, Skull Island: Reign of Kong, Transformers: The Ride, Hollywood Rip Ride Rockit, Revenge of the Mummy, Harry Potter and the Escape from Gringotts,* and *Men in Black: Alien Attack.*

Child Swap

Sometimes when visiting a theme park, two adults may want to ride an attraction but have a child that is not tall enough.

Universal Orlando has a solution that allows you to take turns riding, but only queue once – Child Swap.

Simply ask a Team Member at an attraction entrance to use Child Swap.

Each ride works a little differently, but generally one or more adults will go in the standard queue line while another adult is directed to a child swap waiting area.

Once the first group has queued up and ridden the attraction, they proceed to the Child Swap area. Here the first group will stay with the child, and the person who sat with the child gets to ride straight away, without having to wait in the queue line.

This procedure may vary between attractions – make sure you ask the Team Member at each attraction entrance about the specific procedure.

The Universal Orlando app

The Official Universal Orlando Resort App, available for free on smartphones, allows you to access wait times for all attractions when inside the parks, get directions to attractions with step-by-step visual representations, see show times and special events, get custom wait time alerts, see park and resort maps, find guest amenities, see park hours, set show time alerts, share on social media, and locate food items.

Universal Orlando has said that in the future it will add new features such as instant Express Pass purchases and customizable itineraries. The app is available for free for Apple and Android devices.

Package delivery

Universal Orlando's package delivery service allows you to purchase any item and have it stored until later in the day when you can pick it up. This means you won't have to carry it around all day.

You can choose to have your purchase sent to on of two locations:

• The front of the park – By each of the theme parks' exit turnstiles you will see a small shop that is accessible both from inside and outside the park. Purchases made throughout the day will be sent here for you to pick up. Allow 4 hours for delivery here.
• Your hotel room – You can also have the package delivered straight to your hotel room if you are staying at one of the on-site hotels. The only caveat is that it will be delivered the next day between 9:00am and 4:00pm. This service is unavailable the day before checkout or the day of checkout itself, so it is only suitable for stays of 3 nights or more.

Q-Bot Ride Reservation System

Q-Bot is a ride reservation scheme that is a more affordable alternative to Express Pass. The Q-Bot system is available anywhere that Express Pass can be purchased and is valid on all Express Pass rides, but it cannot be used for shows.

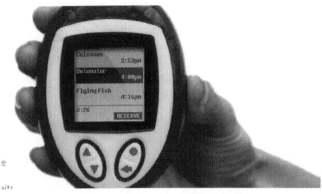

The system is managed on a portable device called a Q-Bot, which you rent for the duration of the day. It allows you to make ride reservations – the Q-Bot is not a front of the line access system.

How does it work?

Unlike the Express Pass, this system does not get you onto rides any faster; instead it allows you to virtually reserve a place in line. For example: The time is currently 14:00 and the line for *Revenge of the Mummy* is 40 minutes.

You select *Revenge of the Mummy* on your Q-Bot and make a reservation – in this example the reservation would be for 14:40 (the current time plus the wait time).

At 14:40, you can return to the attraction and enter through the Express Pass line – this line will get you onto the ride quickly but may take up to 15 minutes during peak periods.

While you are waiting for your reservation time, you can go and experience another attraction or show in the regular queue line, shop, eat, etc.

Used efficiently, you can double the number of rides you experience per day and spend a lot less time in queue lines.

Our favorite way to use the Q-bots is to make a reservation for a ride and then use that time to watch a show – this way you don't feel like you are waiting at all.

One great feature of the Q-Bot is that you can make ride reservations on the device wherever you are in the park, without needing to be physically present at an attraction to reserve. This means, for example, that you could be having lunch and make a reservation for *Despicable Me: Minion Mayhem*.

Do not cancel your reservation as you walk up to each attraction, the ride operator will validate your Q-Bot and then allow you access to the Express Pass queue.

For rides where you must stow your belongings in lockers, go to the ride entrance first, the ride attendant will validate your Q-Bot and you will be given a slip of paper to return to the Express Pass queue with, after you have stowed your belongings (including the Q-Bot).

Cancelling reservations:
You may cancel reservations at any time on the device, and you can have one active reservation at a time.

In order to create another reservation, you must ride the attraction or cancel a reservation.

Going back to our previous example, you can ride *Revenge of the Mummy* any time after 14:40. If it is 14:40 or later and you have still not used your *RoTM* reservation, you cannot reserve another ride until you ride *RoTM* or cancel the reservation.

If you cancel a reservation, it is the equivalent of you leaving the queue line – you lose your place, and if you later want to reserve for the same ride, you must wait the full wait time.

What are my options?
There are two versions of Q-Bot – one allows one reservation per ride, the other allows unlimited reservations so you can make multiple reservations for the same ride.

Is it worth it?
Given the option of Express Passes and the Q-Bot and an unlimited supply of money, of course the Express Passes win, as you get on rides in a maximum of 15 minutes – and usually in less than 5. However, if you have a more limited budget, and do not like waiting in lines, then this may work well for you.

To make the most of this system, we recommend making Q-Bot reservations for the rides with the longest waits rather than those with shorter waits.

If you are visiting both parks in one day, and want to skip the lines at both, you will need to purchase one Q-Bot at each park which is a lot of hassle. We recommend an Express Pass in this case, despite the extra cost.

Note 1: Q-Bot is not offered every day of the year. There are days when only Express Passes are sold.

Note 2: When you purchase Q-Bot access, you will receive a voucher to be exchanged elsewhere. There, you will sign a contract stating you will return the device, and provide credit or debit card payment details. You cannot use the Q-Bot system without a credit or debit card. If the Q-Bot is not returned or is damaged, you will be charged $50.

Stoller and Wheelchair Rentals

Both theme parks offer stroller, wheelchair and motorized ECV rentals. The rental area is located to the left hand side of each park's turnstiles.

Rentals are priced as so (per day):

*Single Stroller – $15
*Single Kiddie Car – $18
*Double Stroller – $25
*Double Kiddie Car – $28
*Wheelchairs – $12, plus a $50 deposit.
*ECVs – $50plus a $50 deposit.

The kiddie car is a stroller designed to look like a car with an enclosed front foot area, to stop kids slipping out. It also has a steering wheel to play with.

ECVs must be operated by a single person aged 18 years old or over. Wheelchairs can also be rented in the parking rotunda area.

Guests with Disabilities

Visiting a theme park can be a complicated process for someone with a disability, but Universal Orlando has worked hard to give people in this situation as much of the full theme park experience as possible. Although, we could not possibly cover every kind of disability in this section, we have tried to include as much information as possible.

Universal Attraction Assistance Pass

A Universal Attraction Assistance Pass can really ease the day for some visitors. In order to obtain it, you will need to go to Guest Services (to the right through the turnstiles) and ask for the Attraction Assistance Pass.

Although it is not required, we strongly recommend you get a note from your doctor in English explaining what exactly you need help with - whether it is avoiding waiting in the sun, standing for prolonged periods of time, or waiting in crowded areas. It will all depend on your situation. Your doctor does NOT need to explain what your disability is, merely what help you require in the theme parks.

The Universal Team Members at Guest Services will ask you several question to determine eligibility and what type of help you require. As mentioned before, a doctor's letter is not required but will greatly assist this process. You will then be issued an Attraction Assistance Pass and it will be explained to you.

Using the pass:
When you reach an attraction you would like to ride, show your Assistance Pass to the Team Member at the ride entrance (the attraction 'greeter').

If the attraction's wait time is less than 30 minutes, then you will be immediately directed towards an alternative queue; this is often the Express Pass queue line.

If the attraction's wait time is more than 30 minutes, then the greeter will write down a time on your Pass to return – we will call this a 'reservation' for the purpose of this guide.

When that time comes around, show your pass with the reservation time at the ride entrance to be granted entry through the alternative queue. Remember that this is

NOT a front-of-the-line ticket and waits can still be up to 15 minutes.

You can only hold one ride 'reservation' at any one time.

You may still enjoy accelerated entrance to attractions with less than a 30-minute wait, even if you have an active reservation.

If you want to change which attraction you have a reservation for, simply go to the next attraction and make a reservation with the attraction's greeter at the entrance. This will automatically void your previous reservation.

An Assistance Pass allows up to 25 reservations, which should be more than enough for a single day.

The Assistance Pass is valid for up to 6 people in the person's party.

Express Guest Assistance Pass:
The Express Guest Assistance Pass is used in situations when waiting in any form of queue or having to return later is simply not possible, making the classic Universal Attractions Assistance Pass not suitable.

As such, this pass is aimed at a much more limited number of guests and it is more difficult to obtain. This Pass does not require proof with a doctor's note, but a note can help. You may need to ask to speak to a manager to obtain this card.

Generally speaking, the Express Guest Assistance Pass is for guests with certain mental health disorders, though a list of eligibility is not officially disclosed.

This Pass will allow you to enter the alternative queue instantly without needing to obtain a return time, no matter what the wait time is. This is NOT a front-of-the-line ticket and you must wait in the alternative queue.

The Express GAP is not valid at *Harry Potter and the Escape from Gringotts* and the *Hogwarts Express* at *Universal Studios Florida*. It is also not valid at *Harry Potter and the Forbidden Journey*, the *Hogwarts Express*, and *Pteranodon Flyers* at *Islands of Adventure*.

If you wish to visit the above rides, then a classic Attraction Assistance Pass is necessary, or you will need to use the regular queue line instead. Overall, this Pass acts very similarly to the Universal Express Pass Unlimited.

Other Accommodations for Disabled Guests

Deaf/Hard of Hearing – For guests who are deaf or hard of hearing, many in-park shows have interpreted performances. The timings of these shows are printed on the regular park map.

Closed captioning and assistive listening devices, guidebooks for guests with disabilities, and attraction scripts are also available at Guest Services in each theme park.

Mobility Impairment and Wheelchairs – The whole of Universal Orlando has been designed to be as wheelchair-accessible as possible with ramps instead of steps. All shopping and dining facilities are accessible. Guests who would like to use a stroller as a wheelchair should ask for a special tag from Guest Services.

Outdoor stage shows also have designated areas for wheelchair users and their parties.

Most rides are accessible – some will require a transfer; others will allow you to ride in your wheelchair.

You can get a wheelchair at the parking rotunda to help with the considerable distance from the rotunda to the theme parks if necessary – simply ask the Team Members here. Alternatively, you can rent these inside the theme parks.

Guests may pay the additional cost for an ECV once at the theme park or continue to use the wheelchair throughout the day.

You do not NEED to have an Attraction Assistance Pass if you are in a wheelchair as all rides have an accessible entrance, but it can make things easier when there are particularly long queues, so we do recommend it.

If you, or someone you are with, suffers from a disability that is not easily seen we thoroughly recommend the use of one of the Assistance Passes – without one you will need to use the regular queue line.

Service Animals are permitted throughout the theme parks but each attraction will have a specific way of boarding. Kennels are available at some attractions for service animals.

The greeters at the entrance of each attraction are able to provide more information.

Rides and shows: Special restrictions apply to guests with prosthetic limbs and guests with oxygen tanks.

More information about rides and shows specifically is available through the Riders Guide for Rider Safety & Guests with Disabilities (PDF file). It can be downloaded online from http://bit.ly/uordisab.

Dining

When visiting the Universal Orlando Resort you will find an abundance of food choices, from standard Quick Service theme park fare to fine dining. However, eating somewhere you have never visited can lead to some uncertainty, especially for picky eaters, so this chapter aims to help.

Quick Service Universal Dining Plan

Guests wishing to plan their meal budget in advance may want to consider one of Universal's dining plans.

The Quick Service Universal Dining Plan is available to all guests and can be bought at any theme park Quick Service location, at UniversalOrlando.com or at dining reservation kiosks in the parks. It is accepted at over 100 locations at the Universal Orlando Resort.

Pricing
The cost of the Quick Service dining plan is $21.99 + tax for adults and $13.99 + tax per child.

What is included?
Each day purchased on the Universal Quick Service Dining Plan entitles you to:
• 1 Quick Service meal – with Entrée and Non-alcoholic beverage.
• 1 Snack – From food carts or Quick Service locations such as popcorn, ice cream or a frozen beverage.
• 1 Non-Alcoholic Beverage – From food carts or Quick Service locations.

You will receive a voucher when you reserve your dining plan that can be exchanged for a dining plan card at the Ticket Centre or Guest Services at either theme park, or the Dining Reservation Cart at either theme park or *CityWalk*.

The Quick Service Dining Plan can be redeemed at all food locations owned and operated by Universal Orlando in *Universal Studios Florida* and *Islands of Adventure*, and at select *CityWalk* locations including *Hot Dog Hall of Fame* and *Bread Box*.

Is it worth the price?
In our opinion, the Quick Service plan is not going to be a great purchase if you are looking for value for money, as you would really have to try hard to profit from this dining plan and you would need to choose the most expensive entrées on the menu every time.

Also, this isn't what we would classify as a real dining plan, as there is only one actual meal included – the rest are drinks and snacks. This will likely not be enough for most people.

If, however, you want to have meals paid for in advance then you may enjoy this option.

Top Tip: You can add a Coca-Cola Freestyle cup to this plan for $6 extra per day - this gives you unlimited soda refills for the day. More on these cups later in this chapter.

Universal Dining Plan

Unlike the Quick Service Universal Dining Plan, the Universal Dining Plan is only available to guests who have booked a vacation package through Universal Parks & Resorts Vacations or an authorized reseller – this includes both on-site and off-site hotels. The Dining Plan cannot be purchased at the theme parks.

The cost of the dining plan is $55.99 + tax for adults and $18.99 for children (aged 3 to 9).

Each day on the Dining Plan entitles you to:
• 1 Table Service meal – with Entrée, Dining Plan Dessert and Non-alcoholic beverage.
• 1 Quick Service meal – with Entrée and Non-alcoholic beverage.
• 1 Snack – From food carts or Quick Service locations such as popcorn, ice cream or a frozen beverage.
• 1 Beverage – From food carts or Quick Service locations.

For those familiar with the Disney Dining Plan at Walt Disney World, this is very similar but there is one crucial difference: whereas at Disney you have to purchase a Dining Plan for the entire stay, (e.g.

At Disney an 8-day stay would mean purchasing an 8-day Dining Plan), at Universal you buy however many days' worth of credits you need. So it would be possible to purchase 3 days' worth of food during an 8-day stay.

You must purchase the plan for every member of your family aged over two years old.

Credits are available for your entire stay. For example, with a 3-day dining package you would get 3 Table Service meal credits, 3 Quick Service meal credits, 3 Snack credits and 3 beverage credits.

With the Universal Dining Plan, you could split these between several days throughout

the entire duration of your stay. You could have a Table Service meal one day and a snack, and then have two Quick Service meals another day.

Character fans can use one Table Service credit for the *Superstar Character Breakfast* at *Cafe La Bamba*.

The Universal Dining Plan can be redeemed at most food locations owned and operated by Universal Orlando in *Universal Studios Florida* and *Islands of Adventure*, and at select *CityWalk* locations - a full list follows. On-site hotel restaurants are not on the Dining Plan.

Guests who purchase the Dining Plan will receive a voucher when you book their vacation to be exchanged in the theme parks or *CityWalk*. The voucher can be exchanged for a card at the Ticket Centre Desk or Guest Services at either theme park, or Dining Reservation Carts at either theme park or *CityWalk*. It can also be collected at on-site hotels.

For an extra $20 per adult or $7 per child, you can use one Table Service credit for the *Cinematic Spectacular Experience* at *Lombard's Seafood Grille*.

Is it worth it?
The Dining Plan is a good option for food lovers, but compared to Disney's system it still has a few niggles to work out. Firstly, exchanging a voucher given at booking for a card is time consuming.

Secondly, Dining Plan restaurants in *CityWalk* are limited – all the other restaurants are inside the theme parks, so you will need park admission each day. Frustratingly, as the on-site hotels are operated by Loews and not Universal, on-site hotel restaurants are not included in the plan.

Thirdly, each card has its own credits and operates independently. As such, a parent wanting to get four ice creams needs all four cards, and each ice cream is processed separately. Credits are not grouped like the Disney Dining Plan.

Having mentioned all these caveats, it *is* a good system. If you like having all your meals pre-paid with one less expense to worry about, and enjoy Table Service meals, then this is the perfect plan for you.

This plan generally offers better value than the Quick Service dining plan, especially if you eat the most expensive items on the menus, meaning that you can save money here.

Note: Gratuities are not included in the price of the Dining Plan.

WHERE CAN I USE MY DINING PLAN?

Universal Studios Florida:
Snacks – *San Francisco Pastry Company*
Quick Service – *Beverly Hills Boulangerie, Fast Food Boulevard, KidZone Pizza Company, Leaky Cauldron, London Taxi Hut, Louie's Italian Restaurant, Mel's Drive In, Richter's Burger Co.,* and *Universal Studios' Classic Monsters Café.*
Table Service – *Finnegan's Bar and Grill* and *Lombard's Seafood Grille*
Character Dining – *Superstar Character Breakfast at Café La Bamba*

Islands of Adventure:
Quick Service – *Blondie's, Cafe 4, Captain America Diner, Circus McGurks Cafe Stoopendous, Comic Strip Café, Croissant Moon Bakery, Fire Eater's Grill, Green Eggs and Ham Café, The Burger Digs, Three Broomsticks, Thunder Falls Terrace* and *Wimpy's.*
Table Service – *Mythos Restaurant* and *Confisco Grille and Backwater Bar*
Character Dining – *The Grinch & Friends Character Breakfast (Seasonal)*

CityWalk:
Snacks – *Auntie Anne's Pretzels, Blue Man Group Theater Coke, Cold Stone Creamery and Icon Hub Cart* and *Starbucks Coffee.*
Quick Service – *Bread Box Hand Crafted Sandwiches, Cinnabon, Hot Dog Hall of Fame, Menchie's Frozen Yogurt* and *Red Oven Pizza Bakery*
Table Service – *Antojitos Authentic Mexican Food, Bob Marley: A Tribute to Freedom, Jimmy Buffet's Margaritaville, NBA City, Pat O' Brien's, The Cowfish* and *Vivo Italian Kitchen.*

Refillable Drinks and Popcorn

Popcorn:
Refillable popcorn buckets are a great way to get a snack in if you are a big eater. You first pay $5.99 for the popcorn bucket, and then can get as many refills as you want for $1.29 plus tax each.

There are four places at each theme park where your souvenir bucket can be refilled: just look for the big popcorn machines – these are usually outdoors. There are no popcorn refills at *CityWalk*, or at the on-site hotels.

Popcorn refills are only available for standard popcorn; flavored popcorn is not discounted and must be purchased at full price.

Coca Cola Freestyle:
Coca Cola Freestyle machines are a refillable drinks option that works in a different manner to the previous scheme.

Here, you pay $12.99 plus tax for a Coca Cola Freestyle cup. You can then visit any of the 8 Coca Cola Freestyle locations - 4 in each park (all in Quick Service restaurants, bar one at *Islands of Adventure*) and refill your cup for free as many times as you want during that day. The cup has an RFID chip that, when activated, allows free refills.

There are over 100 different Coke drink mixes you can choose from at the machines, or you can stick to the standard Coke products.

As you must wait ten minutes between refills with Coca Cola Freestyle, this discourages sharing. Additional days can be added for $5.99 per day.

Coke Freestyle stations at *CityWalk* and at Universal's on-site hotels cannot be used with this system.

Dining Reservations

Dining at the Universal Orlando Resort is varied, with options ranging from Quick Service meals to full-blown Table Service locations.

When you want to sit down and have a meal in a busy theme park, you do not want to be kept waiting and you want to make sure there is a seat reserved for you. Each minute you wait could be used to meet characters, watch shows or ride attractions. This is where dining reservations come in.

Unlike some of the other theme parks in the area (such as Disney), at Universal you will not have trouble making dining reservations. There is no need to sit by your computer 180 days before you want your meal either.

Simply browse through the various restaurants and their menus on the Universal Orlando website, and book your table via OpenTable, whenever you want, at no cost to you.

With the exception of very busy seasons, you should be able to get a reservation for almost every restaurant even 4 or 5 days in advance.

If there is a specific place you want to eat, we recommend you book your table as early as possible. However, we have frequently decided that we would like to eat a particular location and have known to get reservations on the very same day.

If you do want to book in advance, then the official Universal website is the place to go. You will need to visit www.universalorlando.com/Restaurants/50-Great-Restaurants.aspx.

We do not recommend going directly to the OpenTable website as you cannot find all the restaurants at the resort on one page.

BUTTERBEER TOP TIPS

Butterbeer is *The Wizarding World of Harry Potter*'s signature drink and can be found in regular ($4.99), hot ($4.99) or frozen ($5.99) varieties.

Souvenir mugs can be purchased for an extra $9 – these do not provide discounted refills on Butterbeer, but do for most other drinks.

Top Tip 1: If you are thinking of getting a Butterbeer in Hogsmeade, go to the Hog's Head to get it. The queue lines are usually much shorter than from the dedicated Butterbeer carts outside and it is a fantastic place to relax.

Top Tip 2: If you want a Butterbeer in Hogsmeade at the start of the day then you will want to get it from the cart by Hogwarts Castle and not the one in Hogsmeade village opposite Dragon Challenge. The lines will be shorter.

Top Tip 3: In our opinion, even better than regular or frozen Butterbeer, is the new amazingly tasty Butterbeer ice-cream that you can get from Florean Fortescue's Ice-Cream Parlour in Diagon Alley. Try it!

Top 5 Table Service Restaurants

Universal has Table Service restaurants dotted across its theme parks, *CityWalk* and the on-site hotels, so finding the best one can be a bit of a task. Luckily, we have rounded up those that you really should not miss out on below.

Note that prices and menus change all the time with seasons and chefs - those which we have listed were correct as of when we last ate at the locations and should merely be taken as examples.

1. Mythos (Islands of Adventure) – *Mythos* is often rated as the number one theme park restaurant in all of Orlando, let alone just Universal. *Mythos* is a pure delight to eat in, with its lavish interior, exotic menu and rather fair prices. This restaurant will truly transport you to a different world.

Entrées are priced between $10 and $22. The food ranges from sandwiches to Shortribs, Asian Salmon and Mahi Mahi. Note: *Mythos* is often only open for lunch.

2. Finnegan's Bar and Grill (Universal Studios Florida) – *Finnegan's* is always a fun place to dine in, or to simply go inside for a quick drink. Themed as an Irish Pub, there is a lot of fun to be had, as well as some delightful treats.

Entrées are priced between $10 and $22. The food includes sandwiches, Fish 'n' Chips, Beef Stew and Sirloin Steak.

3. Confisco Grille & Backwater Bar (Islands of Adventure) – Located in the *Port of Entry* area, *Confisco Grille* has a more traditional range of theme park food, which may be better for families with younger children who are not quite ready to eat the Mahi Mahi at *Mythos*. It also has a more laid-back atmosphere.

Entrées are priced between $9 and $22. You will find wood-oven pizzas, sandwiches, pasta, fajitas and more on the menu.

4. NBA City (CityWalk) – Many ignore this restaurant when walking past, perhaps discounting it as tacky because of its basketball theme. Do not be one of the people that makes that mistake; NBA City has some great food on offer and the portions are huge! The desserts in particular are to die for – try the Cinnamon Berries and the fried Cheesecake for an unforgettable end to a meal.

Entrées are priced between $10 and $34. There is a wide selection of food on offer from chicken quesadillas to pizzas, jambalaya, shrimp, salmon, pasta, and much more.

5. Emeril's (CityWalk) – *Emeril's* is the most premium of the Table Service restaurants listed here, with prices to match. With New Orleans-inspired dishes, you can enjoy seeing your food be prepared in the open kitchen. Alternatively, indulge and book yourself into the Chef's private tasting room with space for ten people.

Entrées are priced between $12 and $18 for lunch, and $24 to $30 for dinner. Food ranges from shrimps and grits, calamari, lasagne and the 18-oz ultimate rib-eye steak.

Top 5 Quick Service Restaurants

There are times that you may not want a three-course meal, preferring to use the time to watch a show, walk around the parks or ride your favorite attraction again.

Here are our favorite on-site Quick Service restaurants to make the most of your park time.

1. Three Broomsticks (Islands of Adventure)
– Everything about this restaurant puts on the top of the pile: the atmosphere, the food and its opening hours. *Three Broomsticks* is open for breakfast, lunch and dinner, and is the only restaurant at *The Wizarding World of Harry Potter - Hogsmeade*.

Entrées are priced between $8 and $15. Breakfast entrées come from around the world: English, American and Continental Europe just to name a few.

Lunch and dinner revolves around British dishes with some American classics too. You will find Cornish pasties, fish & chips, shepherd's pie, as well as smoked turkey legs, rotisserie smoked chicken and spareribs.

2. Thunder Falls Terrace (Islands of Adventure)
– This is another restaurant where the atmosphere adds to the experience. Step foot into *Thunder Falls* and you are in the middle of the world of Jurassic Park - and you get a spectacular view of the *River Adventure* ride splashdown from the restaurant's huge glass windows.

Entrées are priced between $9 and $16. You will find cheeseburgers on sale, as well as ribs, smoked turkey legs, wraps, and rotisserie chicken. The portion sizes are large.

The rotisserie chicken has been dry every time we have eaten here, but the ribs are great!

3. Louie's Italian Restaurant (Universal Studios Florida) – As far as pizzas and pasta are concerned for inside the theme parks, *Louie's* does it best. It should be noted that there is not a huge variety of food on offer at Louie's and it is not particularly healthy.

Entrées are $6 to $14. You can also order a full pizza pie to share for $29 to $36. Food on offer includes spaghetti and meatballs, pizza and fettuccine alfredo. The meatballs and pizzas the best we've had at a theme park Quick Service location.

4. Leaky Cauldron (Universal Studios Florida) – This location has a great atmosphere inside, and like its other *Wizarding World* companion in this section, you can get some good British grub including Banger's and Mash, Cottage Pie, Toad in the Hole, Fish and Chips, etc. Entrées are $9 to $20.

5. Croissant Moon Bakery (Islands of Adventure) – The food here is far from your standard theme park fare. This is a bakery and not somewhere to go for a full-blown lunch or dinner meal, but where you might go for breakfast or a snack.

Croissant Moon is not listed on the theme park map; you will find it in *Port of Entry*. Entrées are $2.50 to $10. This location serves continental breakfasts, sandwiches, Paninis and delicious cakes! If you fancy a coffee, this is the place to visit too!

Tips, Savings and More

This section covers various ways to make your trip better - from ways to save time and money, to Early Park Admission and character meets.

Money Saving Tips

Bring food from home
Universal allows you to bring your own food into the parks, so why not do exactly that?

Whether it is a bag of chocolates or a drink, you can purchase these items at a fraction of the price anywhere outside of Universal property.

For drinks, why not put them in a cooling bag (hard-sided coolers are not allowed in the parks), and/or freeze them to drink throughout the day. Food should be fine in a backpack throughout the day. Glass containers and bottles are not permitted in the parks.

Bring rain gear
There is a high likelihood that at some point during your Universal Orlando theme park adventure you will get wet, whether on one of the water rides, or in one of the famous Floridian thunderstorms.

Either way, we recommend you bring rain protection from

home - either a raincoat, a poncho or even an umbrella (be aware of lightning and umbrellas though).

This saves you 1) from purchasing these items in the theme parks at inflated prices, and 2) buying new clothes when you get soaked.

Those big human dryers outside the water rides that you can pay $5 to go into are not very effective – do not waste your money.

Buy tickets in advance
Whatever you do, do not buy tickets at the gate – you will waste time and pay more than you need to.

As you are reading this guide, we can safely assume that you will be doing some planning before you go, so there is no excuse not to buy your tickets in advance.

You can do this over the phone, online at www.universalorlando.com or through a third party. You will save at least $20 per multi-day ticket

by pre-purchasing them.

What's more, if you buy these tickets through the official Universal Orlando Resort website, you will receive a coupon booklet with up to $150 in money-off coupons.

In addition, certain countries can get special deals, such as the UK where there is a 14-day ticket for the price of a standard 2-day two-park ticket on the official UK Universal Orlando website.

You do not NEED an Express Pass
By following our Touring Plans, you will be able to see the majority of both Universal Parks in two days, so if you that amount of time, Express Pass simply is not needed: you can save up to $150 per person on Express Passes alone.

If you want to do everything in one day, Express Passes are a must.

If you want Express Passes, stay on-site

The on-site hotels are more expensive than those off-sit, but staying at select on-site hotels gets you unlimited Express Passes for everyone in the room for the duration of your stay, including check in and check out days.

To make the most of this, simply book a one-night stay at a Universal hotel.

On your check-in day, despite the fact your room will only be available from 3:00pm onwards, you can actually check in at any time and leave your bags and receive your Express Passes.

This means you can theoretically get there at 7:00am or 8:00am, check in and head straight to the parks.

On your checkout day your Express Passes are valid until theme park closing, even after you check out. Express Passes are included in rooms at the *Hard Rock Hotel, Royal Pacific Resort* and *Portofino Bay Resort*.

Stay off-site

If you are on a budget, then stay off-site. There are many hotels that are only just off Universal Orlando Resort property – a two to three-minute drive away, or a 15-minute walk. These rooms can cost a fraction of the price of the on-site hotels. Plus, at the on-site hotels you will have to pay a nightly parking fee, which may be the case off-site.

Loyalty cards

AAA members, American Express Card holders and UK-based AA members can all receive different discounts throughout the resort.

The AAA/AA discount is usually 10% at restaurants, though be sure to ask for it any time you pay for anything.

Ride photos

Universal are pretty strict on you not taking photos of the monitors showing your on-ride photos.

As such, we recommend purchasing a Universal Photo Package – see the 'Services' chapter for more on this. It will pay for itself if you plan on buying just a few ride photos.

Stay at a partner hotel

Stay at one of Universal Orlando's partner hotels to receive in-room coupons, and depending on who you book it with, you may get Early Park Admission too.

Free lockers

Universal charges for lockers on water rides but not on any other rides. Would they know for example if you put your belongings in another ride's lockers that are free and then walked over to the water ride? No.

If you will be doing this, be prepared to do a lot of walking to save a few dollars. Also be prepared to look around for the ride with the longest wait times to store your belongings in. Both *Harry Potter and the Forbidden Journey* and *Dragon Challenge* often have lockers with long access times.

Get *CityWalk* coupons

There is a completely free coupon book offering savings all across *CityWalk*.

You can get it from the small kiosk near the elevator between the two floors of *CityWalk*. You can also get dining information here.

Vouchers from here are generally for food, and offers vary throughout the year.

How to Spend Less Time Waiting In Line

Park opening
Make sure you get to the theme park well before it officially opens. Ideally, you should be at the gate 30 minutes or more before opening. Remember it will take some time to park your car and get to the theme parks too.

Early morning is the least busy time of the day, and in the first hour you can usually do three or four of the biggest rides, something that would take several hours during the day.

The parks are also often opened earlier than advertised, particularly during busy periods.

Use Single Rider lines
If you do not mind riding separately from the rest of your party, take advantage of the Single Rider queue lines. See our chapter dedicated to these. They will reduce your wait time significantly, meaning you can experience more things per day; they are available at a surprisingly large number of major attractions.

Touring Plans
We have expertly crafted Touring Plans that tell you what order to do the attractions in; these have been crafted to let you see as much as possible while spending as little time as possible in queues.

Parades and Fireworks
If you have a desire to get onto rides and no desire to see parades or fireworks, then use the time the shows are on to visit the big rides, as crowds dwindle during these big events.

Parades
Do not ride attractions near the parade route immediately after the parade; they will be busier than usual.

The 59-minute rule
If Universal closes its parks at 9:00pm, that is when the queue lines (not the rides) close. Anyone in the queue line at park closing time will be allowed to ride, no matter how long the line is.

This means that if you have one final ride to do and it is getting to park closing time, get into the queue line before the park closes and you will still be able to ride.

This rule may not apply if an attraction has an exceptionally long line that would cause it to keep running for hours after the park closing time.

Early Park Admission

How do you fancy being able to get into the theme parks before other guests? Benefit from much shorter queue lines at select attractions, and an emptier park, with Universal's Early Park Admission (EPA).

During most of the year, Universal Orlando Resort offers one hour early entry to one of the two theme parks. This benefit is available to on-site hotel guests and guests who have booked a Universal Vacation Package. It is available daily including check-in and check-out days.

At *Islands of Adventure* you will be able to access *The Wizarding World of Harry Potter: Hogsmeade* including all attractions (except *Hogwarts Express* which opens when *Universal Studios Florida* starts its operating day). *Caro-Seuss-el* in *Seuss Landing* is also available to ride.

At *Universal Studios Florida*, you can access *The Wizarding World of Harry Potter: Diagon Alley* and its attractions, minus the *Hogwarts Express*, which opens at the same time as *Universal's Islands of Adventure. Despicable Me: Minion Mayhem* is also available for Early Park Admission.

Early entry is offered daily for on-site hotel guests. It is also offered with vacation packages booked through Universal whether staying on-site or not, as long as you have booked through Universal and purchased accommodation and park tickets together.

The park open for Early Park Admission is usually announced in advance on the website. This website may change or update as your trip approaches. During busier periods, both parks may be open early.

How do I get Early Park Admission?

Guests staying at on-site Universal hotels must show their room key to gain early admission to the parks.

If this is on your arrival date, then make sure you check in before Early Admission starts and then go over to the parks; your room will not be ready but you will have Early Access to one or both parks.

You may be sent a text message with your room number later on. If you do not receive it, simply stop by the front desk to get your room number.

Guests with a Universal Vacation Package staying off-site do not need to check in to their hotel room, simply go straight to the Will Call kiosks located by the entrance to each park.

Here you can enter your confirmation number given to you when booking to redeem your tickets with Early Park Admission.

We advise you bring your travel confirmation sent to you when you booked the package. This proves that you are entitled to this benefit in case there are any problems at the turnstiles.

Early entry is one hour before regular park opening – that is 8:00am most of the year (with the parks opening for regular guests at 9:00am), and 7:00am during peak seasons.

Character Meet and Greets

Meeting characters can be one of the most enjoyable parts of the day in a theme park for many visitors. Luckily, at Universal Orlando, there are many characters to meet. Usually the characters have little-to-no queues, unlike those at Disney.

At Universal's *Islands of Adventure* in *Marvel Superhero Island*, you will usually find Captain America, Dr. Doom, The Green Goblin, Spider-Man, Storm and Wolverine. They even make their appearances (and disappearances) on cool quad bikes most of the time. You can also meet the Seuss characters at *Seuss Landing* including Cat in the Hat, the Grinch, the Lorax and Thing 1 and 2!

At *Universal Studios Florida* you will find the characters from The Simpsons including Bart, Lisa, Homer, Marge, Krusty the Clown and Sideshow Bob.

You will also find the Blues Brothers, the Men in Black, Shrek, Fiona and Donkey, Barney, SpongeBob, the Minions and Gru, and the Transformers characters regularly in areas outside their respective attractions.

Other characters also occasionally make appearances such as Scooby Doo and Shaggy, Lucy Ball, Woody Woodpecker, Betty Boop, and Marilyn Monroe.

You can check what times characters will be out by looking at your park map. Some characters are not listed on the map such as Scooby Doo but will make periodic appearances in the parks' Character Zones; these are located near the turnstiles at *Universal Studios Florida*, and in *Toon Lagoon* at *Islands of Adventure*.

Operating Hours and Ride Closures

The Universal Orlando Resort is open 365 days a year and park operating hours vary according to demand.

On days when more visitors are expected, the parks are open longer; when there aren't so many, the parks close earlier. The parks always operate for their advertised operating hours.

We strongly advise that you check these in advance of your visit, They may change closer to the date of your visit, so do re-check again.

Park operating hours can be verified up to two months in advance at http://bit.ly/uorhours.

Ride refurbishments also happen throughout the year to keep rides operating safely and efficiently, and rides and attractions must close throughout the year to be renewed. Refurbs tend to avoid the busier times of the year.

Ride closures are only published a month or so in advance on the same page as the opening hours.

Remember that rides may close for technical issues or weather reasons. There is no need to be angry at the ride attendants, as they do not control whether the ride runs or not.

Comparing Universal Orlando and Walt Disney World

Universal is not the only theme park operator in Orlando. Far from it; if it were not for the big competitor in the district, Universal Orlando most likely wouldn't even exist. We are of course referring to the Walt Disney World Resort. There is no doubt that, one day, Universal would like to greet just as many guests as Disney does. Here we compare both resorts, so if you have visited one you can learn about the other.

Resort Size

Universal Orlando Resort is a needle in a haystack when compared to Walt Disney World. Disney covers 47 mi², an area twice the size of Manhattan. Universal Orlando in comparison is about 1 mi² in size. Yes, it is a much smaller resort, but there are both advantages and disadvantages to this.

Walt Disney World hosts four theme parks, two water parks, golf and mini-golf courses, almost thirty resort hotels, miles of roads, lakes, a shopping district and much, much more.

It is also important to note that Disney has only developed one third of its 47 square miles. Even so, Disney's currently developed property real estate is about 15 times larger than Universal's. Universal Orlando Resort has two theme parks, five resort hotels, and a shopping district, which is significantly smaller than Disney's.

This means that Walt Disney World Resort naturally has more things to do; it has the scope to create larger developments – just *Disney's Animal Kingdom Park* alone is about 580 acres in size for example. All of Universal Orlando's land can fit in Animal Kingdom and its parking lot.

This does not mean that Universal has not done a lot with the land it owns. Due to the land restriction Universal has in fact been far more efficient its space.

The sheer size of the resort does also mean that it can take an eternity to get anywhere at the Walt Disney World Resort – you may be staying at an on-site hotel but it could be a 20-minute bus journey to a theme parks.

Whereas, at Universal you are much closer to the action and can catch a boat to the theme parks from most hotels in a matter or minutes, or simply walk everywhere.

Lastly, because of its size you are much more likely to spend one, two or even three weeks at the Walt Disney World Resort, whereas you would struggle to fill more than four or five days at Universal Orlando.

Planning

A visit to Walt Disney World cannot be done without A LOT of planning. You will research the ticket type you need, which of the resort hotels you want to stay at (there are almost thirty to choose from), which theme park you want to visit on which day, and potentially have to book your restaurants 180 days before you even step foot on Disney property.

You then best have a strategy about which rides to do when, know the ins and outs of the Fastpass+ system and know what times the characters meet and greet to make the most of your time – you will even need to make ride reservations 30 to 60 days in advance to get the most out of your visit.

A Universal Orlando Resort vacation does require some planning; we won't lie to you. You know that because you have purchased this guide.

It does, however, not require anywhere near the degree of planning that a Walt Disney World vacation does.

You can take it more at your own pace. There are only five on-site hotels to choose from, though there are many nearby off-site hotels you could consider.

Ticket options are simpler: you simply decide how many days and whether you want to park-hop or not.

Restaurants can be booked much closer to the day or even on the day itself, but definitely not 180 days before like at Disney.

As far as having a strategy of what rides and experiences you do

when, we recommend that you have one for all theme parks – Universal Orlando included.

However, you will not need to make ride reservations for Universal Orlando like you do at Disney; this is simply not possible. Follow our touring plans, or if you have Express Pass access, simply enjoy the attractions in whatever order you want.

There is still some planning to do for a Universal Orlando Resort vacation, but it is a lot less than at Walt Disney World.

The Off-Season

Visiting the theme parks during school breaks means that they are going to be busy; the kids are out of school so the theme parks are naturally going to be filled with guests. But what about out of season? Such as September during school time, or February.

At Walt Disney World you can expect to find crowds year round. There are less busy days than others, but there is never going to be a day at Walt Disney World when you can stroll onto *Seven Dwarfs Mine Train* within 5 minutes; it is never going to happen – especially at *Magic Kingdom*.

At Universal Orlando, there are still times of the year in the off-season when almost every ride is a walk-on – these are times when you can experience *Harry Potter and the Forbidden Journey* in a matter or minutes instead of hours! The off-season still exists at Universal.

This has a lot to do with the target demographic of Universal with older teens likely being in school longer, whereas very young kids can visit Disney year-round.

Walt Disney World also appeals more to the local, retired population than Universal Orlando, so it attracts them year-round.

Having said this, if Universal Orlando continues to soar in popularity as it has done in recent years, it is very possible that the same situation will develop, particularly as the parks have a very limited number of attractions.

In 2014, for example, the Universal Orlando Resort theme parks welcomed 7.9% - or 1.2 million - more guests than they did the year prior. In 2013, there was an increase of 1 million guests across the resort.

The parks are getting busier at Universal Orlando, just not as busy as at Disney.

Character Meet and Greets

At the Walt Disney World, you need to plan characters meets, even being able to make FastPass+ reservations. At Universal Orlando, its more spontaneous and you almost never have to wait more than 10 minutes to meet a character. Compare that to a 180-minute wait for the princesses at *Magic Kingdom* to see the difference.

Hotel Accommodation and Choice

The on-site hotels at Universal Orlando are physically much closer to the parks than those at Walt Disney World.

However, there are fewer choices and the three top hotels are expensive, though *Cabana Bay* and *Sapphire Falls* offer more moderate pricing.

The flip side is that there are off-site hotels located a 2-minute drive away or a 15-minute walk, for a wider variety of options at Universal.

At Walt Disney World where off-site hotels are a good distance away.

You can actually walk off-site at Universal Orlando and leave the area. You can walk to a Walgreens if you want; you can go and eat outside of the Universal Orlando Resort and make significant savings on the price of food; and reduce the price of accommodation.

This is simply not possible at Walt Disney World without a car, and a lot more hassle.

Innovative Attractions

This one will be controversial for Disney aficionados. In our opinion, Universal is developing more innovative and revolutionary experiences than Disney is nowadays.

Walt Disney World has some incredible experiences of its own - *Test Track, Soarin', Mickey's Philharmagic, Kilimanjaro Safaris, Rock 'n' Rollercoaster,* and the *Tower of Terror* to name but a few.

However, the last big revolution for Disney, in our opinion, was *Expedition Everest* in 2006 – over ten years ago. If we wanted to be generous, *Seven Dwarfs Mine Train* and *Enchanted Tales with*

Belle opened in 2014 and 2012 respectively.

However, in the same timespan, Universal Orlando has blown Disney out of the water. Universal Orlando only opened in 1990 and the resort is dotted with innovative experiences - *The Incredible Hulk Coaster* and *The Amazing Adventures of Spider-Man* win awards year after year. There is *Harry Potter and the Forbidden Journey, Harry Potter and the Escape from Gringotts, Hogwarts Express, Jurassic Park River Adventure, Skull Island: Reign of Kong* and more incredible experiences.

The attractions that have opened at Universal Orlando over

the past few years are immense, and there are new attractions and experiences opening every year for the foreseeable future.

Plus, if you are fan of water rides, whereas *Splash Mountain* at *Disney's Magic Kingdom* may get you a little bit wet, on Universal's water rides you will come out drenched. Universal *Universal's Islands of Adventure* is the perfect place get wet with three major water attractions.

This may all change in 2017 with the opening of Avatar Land at Walt Disney World, but Universal will be counteracting with several attractions, and a water park.

Employees

Although Universal Orlando has recently improved on the friendliness of Team Members, their employees are nothing like Disney's.

Disney's Cast Members are empowered to "make magical moments" to improve vacations in a way Universal employees cannot. Disney employees seem happier, and "courtesy" is one of 4 key values.

At Disney's parks, an employee courtesy is only compromised in safety-critical situations. Otherwise, the Cast Members cannot do enough for you. Most will go above and beyond, and provide exceptional customer service.

Universal Orlando, on the other hand, provides good service and most of the Team Members are great but it seems that all too often these employees are overshadowed by those who are nonchalant at best, or rude at worst. Experiences vary, but Disney has the edge.

Live Entertainment

For a company that is celebrating 100 years of movies Universal you would think that they would know how to put on a good show or two. They do - just not at the Universal Orlando.

Universal Studios Hollywood in California is filled with great shows yet sadly none have made their way across to Orlando.

A rare exception is the live entertainment in *Diagon Alley*, which is outstanding. Shows like *SindBad* and *Fear Factor* are not relevant to the younger generation. In comparison, shows like *Finding Nemo: The Musical* and *Festival of the Lion King* are masterpieces.

It is the same story with parades and fireworks – although better than many other theme parks, Universal's offerings are nowhere near as good as any of Disney's parades or nighttime shows.

Nightlife

In terms of nightlife, Universal Orlando hands down beats Disney. Universal has a wider variety of clubs and bars, and is considered a party scene.

Walt Disney World does not do badly, with bars and a club in *Disney Springs*, but it is just nowhere near the scale of Universal Orlando's offerings.

Both resorts host a large-scale nighttime paid admission show – *Blue Man* at Universal Orlando, and *Cirque du Soleil* at Walt Disney World.

Fastpass+ vs. Express Pass

At Walt Disney World, your park ticket enables you to make free Fastpass+ reservations to skip the regular queue lines by giving you a reserved ride time.

You can make reservations in advance or on the day of your visit – it is a good way of guaranteeing that you will experience some of your favorite attractions.

It is a bit of a complicated system to understand but guidebooks like *The Independent Guide to Walt Disney World 2017* explain the process.

Express Pass at Universal Orlando allows you near-instant entry to almost all attractions for a fee. This fee can be very high and up to $150 per person per day. This is free if you are staying at certain on-site hotels.

Leaving aside that Disney's FastPass+ is much better value as it is free, Universal's Express Pass (because of its paid nature) works better: there is rarely more than a 10-minute wait, you do not make reservations in advance, there is no complicated system to understand, less people use it and it is available for almost every single attraction.

It really is an 'express pass' at Universal Orlando because there's no need to make reservations, you simply turn up and skip the regular queue.

Target Audience

One of the most striking differences between the two resorts is that Universal caters more towards teenagers and adults; Disney has thrill rides but targets families more.

With the exception of rides like *Rock 'n' Rollercoaster, Tower of Terror, Expedition Everest, Mission: SPACE* and *Test Track*, there are few things that will get the adrenaline rushing for teenagers at Disney.

Disney caters more towards families with experiences such as *Soarin', Big Thunder Mountain, Kilimanjaro Safaris* and character meets. At the same time, the small ones can enjoy classics such as *Peter Pan's Flight* and *"it's a small world"*.

Universal Orlando is very different. There are a few things for the younger members of the family, but for the most part it is high intensity thrills that people come to Universal Orlando for, as well as big family adventures. *The Incredible Hulk Coaster, Dueling Dragons, Hollywood Rip Ride Rockit* and *Dr. Doom's Fear Fall* are just a few of the thrill experiences on offer.

Family rides at Universal Orlando are generally more adult-oriented too: *Harry Potter and the Forbidden Journey* and *Harry Potter and the Escape from Gringotts* are most thrilling than most rides at Disney.

There are attractions for smaller kids such as *Barney*, and numerous playgrounds, but there are fewer of these at Universal Orlando.

Special Events

Both Universal and Disney know that ito keep people visiting all year-round, they need seasonal events.

For Halloween, Universal offers a scarier portrayal of the season with *Halloween Horror Nights*, Disney has a "not so scary" approach.

Christmas, however, is a much bigger deal at Walt Disney World than at Universal Orlando, with all four of the theme parks celebrating it through unique shows, decorations, lighting ceremonies and stories from around the world at Epcot.

Even the resort hotels get into the spirit, with Christmas trees and gingerbread houses. Universal Orlando holds its own unique events throughout the year such as *Mardi Gras*.

Disney celebrates the *Flower and Garden Festival*, and the *Food and Wine Festival*. Both resorts celebrate the countdown to the New Year in style.

Dining

Food at Universal Orlando is generally slightly cheaper than at Walt Disney World. There is not as much variety at Universal Orlando as at Walt Disney World though; you will pretty much have to stick to standard theme park food.

The biggest difference in our opinion, however, is the quality and taste; while food at the Disney's parks is not gourmet by any standard, in general, it is much better than Universal Orlando's.

There are also fewer Table Service establishments at Universal Orlando, so sit-down meal options are more limited. At Disney, character buffets and Table Service meals are a big part of the experience.

Resort Transportation

Due to the size of Walt Disney World, there are many ways of getting around, including ferryboats, buses and monorails. Some of these trips make you forget you are at a busy theme park resort.

However, journey times at Walt Disney World Resort can vary from just a few minutes to 25 minutes or more. You may also require several transfers for certain trips. You can also walk between some limited areas of the Walt Disney World Resort, but for the most part, you will need to use the free resort transportation, or drive.

Universal Orlando Resort also allows everyone to use its resort transportation for free. This is made up of a fleet of water taxis, which take you to and from the *CityWalk* area and four of the on-site hotels. The boat journeys should not take more than 10 minutes.

Otherwise, you can use the walking paths throughout the entire Universal Orlando Resort (at Disney many areas do not allow pedestrian traffic), or use the bus transportation.

Seasonal Events

The Universal Orlando Resort offers something different all year round. Whether it is live entertainment, horror mazes or Holiday cheer, the Universal team have it all covered. This section covers all of the seasonal events that happen throughout the year.

A Celebration of Harry Potter
January 27th to 29th 2017

The 'Celebration of Harry Potter' event is three full days of Wizarding fun.

We know nothing except the event date at the time of writing. More information should be available around November 2016. The information in this section pertains to the 2016 event; we expect 2017 to be broadly similar.

Movie stars and autographs:
Several Harry Potter movie stars were present throughout the event.

The 2016 cast included: Rupert Grint (Ron Weasley), Bonnie Wright (Ginny Weasley), Katie Leung (Cho Chang), Matthew Lewis (Neville Longbottom) and Evanna Lynch (Luna Lovegood).

A Celebration of Harry Potter Expo:
Make your way through interactive displays in this unique collection of Harry Potter themed props, movie sets, artwork and more.

• *Harry Potter: The Exhibition* – Be sorted in a Hogwarts-inspired setting. The Exhibition has been on a 7-year, 13-city tour, including a Quidditch.
• *Warner Bros. Studio Tour London: The Making of Harry Potter* – Based at the production home of the Harry Potter movie series, Warner Bros. Studio Tour London is bringing an interactive mini-tour experience to the event, giving you the chance to see the incredible behind-the-scenes talent that went into creating the iconic films.
• *MinaLima* – Graphic designers Miraphora Mina and Eduardo Lima worked for ten years on the Harry

Potter films, creating countless pieces of unforgettable artwork, some of which will be on display, including the Marauder's Map, Daily Prophet, and Hogwarts school books.
• *Pottermore from J.K. Rowling* – Pottermore is the digital heart of the Wizarding World. Keep your eyes peeled for their new Pottermore Correspondent (Rita Skeeter she certainly isn't), who'll be there hunting out exclusive scoops and bringing you updates.
• *Scholastic* – Meet award-winning illustrator Kazu Kibuishi, who re-imagined the Harry Potter book covers.
• *Warner Bros.* – Share a message about what Harry Potter means to you; color in a magical page from the brand-new Harry Potter coloring book; and enter daily raffles for a chance to win books.

Discussions & Demonstrations:

As well as the Expo, guests can enjoy several panels and demonstrations. In 2016, these included:

• *Behind the Scenes: Harry Potter Film Talent Q&A* – Enjoy a fascinating and interactive question and answer session featuring some of your favorite Potter movie actors. Discover what it was like to work on one of the most successful film franchises ever.

• *The Global Impact of Harry Potter: The Exhibition* – Celebrate the touring attraction that has hosted almost 4 million guests. Get an exclusive look at the exhibition's creation and the excitement it continues to deliver to fans around the world. The panel includes exhibition creators, producers, and actors who have participated in the openings.

• *Graphic Design for the Harry Potter Films with MinaLima* – Designers from the graphic design studio MinaLima, share insights into their role as graphic prop designers, and how their paths crossed at the WB film studios to work for 10 years on the Harry Potter movies. They will discuss and show some of the iconic props they created for the Harry Potter films. They will also talk about their recent involvement in *The Wizarding World of Harry Potter - Diagon Alley*, for which they designed all the street and store graphics.

• Harry Potter Props *Showcase with Acclaimed Prop Maker Pierre Bohanna* – Ever wondered how long it takes to make a wand? Or the inspiration for the hundreds of wand designs in the movies? Head prop maker, Pierre Bohanna, will answer these questions and many more. Remember to bring your wand.

Demonstrations For The Younger Fans (Recommended for Ages 12 and Under)

• *Dance Like a Beauxbatons & Battle Like a Durmstrang* – Universal Orlando choreographer will explain the movements and techniques behind the mesmerizing dance routines performed by Beauxbatons and Durmstrang students in the Harry Potter movies.

• *Harry Potter Film Trivia* – Test your Potter knowledge during this fun audience-interaction game inviting younger fans to shout out the answers. Perhaps a Harry Potter marathon is in order before trying your luck?

Mardi Gras
2017 dates to be announced

Celebrate New Orleans with Universal Orlando's Mardi Gras celebrations. The exact dates for 2017 were not available at the time of writing. The event is very similar each year. In 2016, the event ran on select nights from February 6th to April 16th.

Entry to Mardi Gras is included in your regular park admission.

The highlight of the festivities for many is the Mardi Gras Parade with colorful floats and incredible music. Get ready for the traditional throwing of the beads from the floats for you to catch.

Live concerts are the name of the game with the Music Plaza stage hosting live acts on select nights. The line up for 2016 included: Jessie J, Barenaked Ladies, The Fray, Fall Out Boy, Shawn Mendes, T-Pain, and many others.

As well as the bands on the main stage, there are also New Orleans Bands in the French Quarter Courtyard, and stalls with local cuisine including jambalaya and gumbo. This area opens at 4:00pm and closes when concerts start.

There is no seating area for the concerts: it is all general standing room.

For the best view of the Music Plaza Stage concerts, you will need to skip the Mardi Gras Parade altogether or watch it from as close to the Music Plaza stage area as possible.

After the parks are shut, head to the *CityWalk* bars and clubs for more New Orleans fun.

Top Tip: Note that when the parade starts, the regular shows and attractions at the park cease operating.

Important Note: The *Universal Cinematic Spectacular* is not shown on Mardi Gras nights.

Summer Concert Series
Summer 2017 (To Be Confirmed)

Check out big acts in the park while getting some ride time in too. The *Universal Music Plaza* stage area near *Rip Ride Rockit* has bands playing on select dates. There is no extra charge to listen to the live music and there are usually some pretty big bands - all you need is your regular park admission ticket to get in. The concert is standing room only.

It is unclear if you will be able to purchase Concert Only admission to the theme park this year. In the past when this was offered, a concert ticket could be purchased for $69.99 - this allowed you into the park from 7:00pm until park closing. Once inside you can either watch the concert or experience the attractions or a combination of both. Arriving at 7:00pm would not get you front row standing room for the concerts.

Update: In 2016, this event did not run. No official announcement has been made about this concert series for 2017 at the time of writing.

Rock the Universe
September 9th and 10th 2016

Billed as "Florida's Biggest Christian Music Festival", *Rock the Universe* is a whole weekend dedicated to Christian faith and worship, with Christian rock music.

As well as the main stage that features Christian acts, the FanZone features more live music, as well as band autograph sessions, karaoke, and more. On Saturday night, guests can enjoy the Candle-lighting Ceremony.

There is also a free Sunday Morning Worship Service led by a guest speaker for those who hold Rock the Universe tickets. Reservations are required.
Dates for 2017 have not yet been announced

and the line-up is usually released in April each year.

Select attractions will also operate during the Rock the Universe event. In the past these attractions have included *TRANSFORMERS: The Ride-3D, Hollywood Rip Ride Rockit, Revenge of the Mummy, and MEN IN BLACK Alien Attack*. It has been confirmed that *Skull Island: Reign of Kong* will be open for the event in 2016. We do not expect Diagon Alley to be open during this event.

Rock the Universe is a separate ticketed event that operates outside of regular park hours. 2016 tickets are priced at $65.99 for one night of the event, or $103.99 for both nights of the

event. For $99.99 guests can enjoy both an all day ticket on Saturday for either park, plus access to the concert in the evening.

Finally, for $164.99 guests can enjoy both nights of the event plus admission to the park for three full days with park-to-park access for the whole weekend. These tickets offer fantastic value for money.

Top Tip: A one-night event-only Express Pass is available for $25 for one use per participating attraction, or $35 for unlimited uses at participating attractions.

Halloween Horror Nights
Select nights from September 16th to October 31st 2016

This is the biggest event of the year for Universal Orlando and takes place across both coasts - Hollywood and Orlando. It has been running for over 25 years.

Halloween Horror Nights is an evening extravaganza with heavily themed scare mazes (a.k.a. haunted houses), live entertainment and scare zones where "scarectors" roam around frightening guests. The theming is second to none and unlike any other scare attraction in the US. As well all this, you will find most of the regular attractions open inside *Universal Studios Florida*.

Universal warns the event "may be too intense for young children and is not recommended for children under the age of 13". Children under this age may enter as no proof of age is requested but it is not recommended. No costumes or masks are allowed at the event. This nothing like Walt Disney World's "not so scary" Halloween parties. There is no trick-or-treating here; the idea is to be scared.

More information on the 2016 event should be released between July and the end of August 2016.

Halloween Horror Nights (HHN) is very, very popular and *Universal Studios Florida* gets extremely crowded during this events.

On the busiest nights you can expect to wait 90 minutes or more in line for each haunted house. Therefore, we highly recommend purchasing the HHN Express Pass if you want the full experience and to see everything, though it is an additional supplement of over $100 per person. Even with the Express Passes waits can regularly reach an hour, however.

You will likely need to make multiple visits to see everything on offer, especially without Express Passes.

Dates:
The 2016 event will be the biggest ever - spanning 31 nights. Here are the dates the event runs on this year:
September: 16, 17, 18, 22, 23, 24, 25, 29 and 30
October: 1, 2, 6, 7, 8, 9, 12, 13, 14, 15, 16, 19, 20, 21, 22, 23, 26, 27, 28, 29, 30 and 31.

What is part of HHN?
Each year, the entertainment changes at Halloween Horror Nights, and this is one of the things that keeps people coming back

again and again.

For 2016, the following scare houses have been announced:
• Lunatics Playground 3D: You Won't Stand a Chance
• Ghost Town: The Curse of Lightning Gulch
• Tomb of the Ancients
• The Exorcist
• Halloween
• Krampus
• American Horror Story
• The Texas Chainshow Massacre

Guests can expect each house to last about 3 to 5 minutes each.

There are also scare zones in 2016, where characters roam the zones causing fear - here you do not need to queue to be scared. In 2016, these are A Chance In Hell, Dead Man's Wharf, Vamp 1955, Banshee's Lair and Survive or Die.

Also, scattered around the park are scare-actors with chainsaws... ready to run at you.

As far as live stage shows, 2016 sees the return of Bill & Ted's Excellent Halloween Adventure (a really enjoyable stage show) and Academy of Villains: House of Fear.

For the first time ever, in 2016 there is also a new virtual reality experience called "The Repository" - this is a separate upcharge at $50 and is available nightly during HHN.

The following attractions were also open during HHN in 2015: *TRANSFORMERS The Ride 3D, Hollywood Rip Ride Rockit, MEN IN BLACK Alien Attack, Revenge of the Mummy, The Simpsons Ride* and *Escape from Gringotts*.

Queues for attractions are generally non-existent throughout the event, as the focus is on the scare aspect of the night for most people.

Guests with a HHN Express Pass can use it for both the scare mazes and the attractions.

Is The Wizarding World of Harry Potter part of HHN?
Information for the 2016 edition has not been released in regards to this – however, this is how it worked in 2015, we expect it to be similar in 2016:

Halloween Horror Nights entertainment will not extend to the *Wizarding World of Harry Potter: Diagon Alley* area of the park. This means that there will not be any additional 'horror' in Diagon Alley – no scare-actors, no shows, no haunted houses.

However, the area will be open in its normal state meaning that Escape from Gringotts, the shops and the eateries will be open. This will be a safe refuge from the horror outside for anyone that needs a break.

Pricing:
Ticket sales for 2016 are not yet open. For reference, in 2015 a single general admission ticket was priced at $101.99 on the gate or at www.halloweenhorrornights.com/orlando/tickets.html in advance. Think this is expensive? We agree, see the other ticket options below.

HHN as an add on:
You can also add admission to one night of *Halloween Horror Nights* to your daytime park ticket and save a substantial amount of money (versus purchasing them separately).

Your *Halloween Horror Nights* ticket does not have to be used on the same day as your daytime park ticket. The price in 2015 varied between $49.99 and $76.99 depending on the date of your visit. You can buy this in advance with a day ticket, or at the resort itself with a day ticket present with you at the time of purchase.

Rush of Fear Passes:
For online purchases made in advance, the Rush of Fear pass is great value and priced at $83.99. It allows entry to every event night during the first 3 weeks of 2015 for one price. A Rush of Fear + HHN Express Pass option was also available that allowed you entry during the first 3 weeks of 2015 as well as allowing you to bypass the regular lines once at each of the haunted houses every night – this was priced at $229.99.

Other advanced purchase options in 2015 included the Frequent Fear, and Frequent Fear + HHN Express Pass options. These were priced between $94.99 and $297.99, depending on the dates of visit and whether they include Express Pass access or not.

HHN Express passes:
If you wish to buy separate HHN Express Passes, in 2015 these varied in price from $69.99 to $119.99 per person and are valid during the event for haunted houses and attractions. We recommend you buy these in advance as they will sell out for peak nights.

On peak nights you *need* a HHN Express Pass to see everything, as wait times for haunted houses will typically be between 90 minutes and three hours making Express Passes a necessity, not a luxury.

Note that even with an Express Pass, you may have to wait an hour or more to enter the haunted houses during peak nights – it will not be instant or quick entry. Note that Express Passes purchased for daytime at Universal Orlando are not valid during HHN, nor are the Hotel Express Passes – if you want to reduce the waits in queue lines during HHN, you have to cough up some cash.

RIP Tours:
You can get a private VIP tour (dubbed an 'RIP' tour during HHN) with immediate unlimited access to every haunted house and park attraction (plus many other benefits) starting at $1399 for a party of 10. Tax and the cost of HHN park admission are extra.

There are several benefits to this package and if you can get 10 people to do it, $140 each works out at outstanding value for what you get – of course that is the starting price.

If you cannot gather a group, a public RIP tour with one-time immediate access to every haunted house, plus the attractions (plus many other benefits), starts at $139.99 per

person; the cost of park admission is extra.

Daytime Guided Tours:
If you want to see how the horror of HHN is created without the scares, then Universal Orlando offers the Unmasking the Horror Tour.

This tour takes you on a lights-on tour through three haunted houses with a guide. You will learn about the process that goes into creating these houses without the scares. Photos are permitted.

The tour lasts up to 2 hour 30 minutes for groups of up to 15 guests.

Tours are priced at $75 per person (plus tax) and there are both morning and afternoon tours. Both tours go through different haunted houses – guests who wish to see all six houses on the same day can purchase both tours at a discounted price of $130 per person, plus tax. These tours take place during the regular park hours.

You can call to book at 1-866-346-9350 or email vipexperience@ universalorlando.com to book both RIP Tours and the Guided Tour.

HOW TO GET INTO HHN 45 MINUTES EARLY:

You will need to be a day guest to make this work and enter the park with a regular park ticket or annual by 4:15pm. The park usually closes at 5:00pm for regular guests when HHN is on, and guests are not allowed in after 4:30pm.

Next, join one of the queue lines to enter the HHN holding areas: near the *Revenge of the Mummy* and *Finnegan's Bar*, in *Springfield USA*, near *TERMINATOR 2: 3-D*, and in *Diagon Alley*. Up to four of these waiting areas may be open at once. Once in line for one of the holding areas, your HHN ticket will be scanned and you will be given a wristband. You will then wait in this holding area.

At about 5:45pm, 45 minutes before HHN officially begins, you will be allowed to explore the HHN entertainment including the scare houses. Usually only a few of them will be open at this time, but there will be little or no wait, and you can usually experience them all and then explore the rest after 6:30pm when HHN officially starts!

Note that holding are locations may change in 2016. The *Finnegan's Bar* and *Diagon Alley* locations are our favorites.

Grinchmas and the Holiday Season
December

Unlike the season at Walt Disney World which runs from November, the Holiday season at Universal Orlando is shorter. The dates are always similar every year, give or take a few days and it usually runs from the second week in December to early January.

Exact dates for 2016 are not available at the time of writing. The information in this section is from 2015 but the event is broadly similar each year.

Thanksgiving
Although both theme parks do not hold special events for Thanksgiving, the on-site hotels do offer celebrations:
• *Cabana Bay Beach Resort* hosts a dinner and Macy's Thanksgiving Day Parade is shown on big screens at Bayline diner.
• *Loews Royal Pacific Resort* hosts a Holiday buffet with Universal Orlando characters and other live entertainment, priced at $56 per adult and $24 per child. A special Wantilan Luau will take place on the 28th November 2015 with all the regular Polynesian food and

entertainment, plus a special tree lighting ceremony.
• *Hard Rock Hotel Orlando* hosts a Holiday buffet with characters and other live entertainment. This is priced at $58 per adult and $20 for children.
• *Loews Portofino Bay Hotel* offers a buffet in the Tuscan Ballroom with live entertainment, priced at $70 per adult and $26.50 per child. Trattoria del Porto offers a holiday buffet with live entertainment and characters for $63 per adult and $18 per child. Finally, Holiday Harbor Nights is a special event with wine, gourmet food and jazz, as well as an illumination of the resort's main Christmas tree. Tickets start at $45; VIP tickets are $75.

Christmas
At *Universal Studios Florida* watch as the Macy's Holiday Parade rolls through the streets with floats taken from the world-famous full-scale Thanksgiving Day Parade in New York City. This event runs every evening throughout the Holiday season. For the best position, get a spot in the New York area facing the Christmas tree. This is because Santa also lights up the

tree when he goes past.

Top Tip: You can sign up to be a balloon handler and help carry the balloons on the parade route. There are several restrictions as far as being in good health, wearing closed toe shoes, being over 48 inches tall, and being over 18 to participate. Sign up takes place two hours before the parade begins in *Woody Woodpecker's KidZone* next to the teddy bear.

Mannheim Steamroller – the biggest selling Christmas band of all time – rocks the stage with live performances.

In addition, the *A Day in the Park with Barney* show gets a Christmas twist and runs multiple times each day, as does *The Blue's Brothers (Holiday) Show*.

At *Islands of Adventure*, the Holiday fun continues. Watch the fantastic *Grinchmas Who-liday Spectacular* – a 30-minute live-show with music, starring The Grinch himself, telling you the story of how he stole Christmas.

If you fancy something to eat, why not meet the Dr Seuss characters at the Holiday-season-only Character Breakfast with Grinch and Friends - reservations are required.

Finally, you can actually meet The Grinch himself. Play, laugh and get some great photos!

The celebration continues at the on-site hotels. At the resorts, you check out holiday buffets and dining events, tree-lighting ceremonies, special music performances, Hanukkah candle lightings, visits from Santa Claus and Holiday poolside movies.

Unfortunately, there are no meets with Santa Claus at either park throughout the Holiday season. This is a bit of a missed opportunity if you ask us.

New Year's Eve
For the transition into the New Year, head over to *CityWalk* and party the night away with live performances and a midnight champagne toast! This New Year's Eve party is a paid ticketed event.

The New Year's Eve party includes admission to six clubs, six party zones, a pyrotechnics display, unlimited gourmet cuisine, a midnight champagne toast and much more.

It is one of the year's biggest events and tickets run from $105 to $135 per person plus tax. This party is for over 21s only. A VIP package is also available for $145 to $185, plus tax.

Hard Rock Live Orlando hosts its own New Year Eve's party from 8:00pm, priced at $85 to $95 per person; $145 for the VIP package.

The theme parks do not have special entertainment for New Year's Eve but are open late, with *Islands of Adventure* closing at 11:00pm and *Universal Studios Florida* closing at 1:00am. *Universal's Cinematic Spectacular* nighttime show is performed at 11:59pm on New Year's Eve.

The on-site hotels also host their own parties:
• *Cabana Bay Beach Resort* has a complimentary event at Bayline Diner with a balloon drop at midnight, food and drinks, face painting and a DJ. Entry is free but food, drinks, and face painting are extra.
• *Loews Royal Pacific Resort* holds a New Year's Eve Champagne & Cocktail Reception with small bites, a live DJ, a live stream of the ball drop, and a champagne toast. Entry is $38 for adult and $22 per child.

At the New Year's Eve Wantilan Luau, you can celebrate New Year with a buffet, a tree lighting, fire dancers, hula dancers and live music. Pricing is $85 per adult and $35 per child.
• *Hard Rock Hotel* hosts the a party with food and dessert stations, a live stream of Times Square, a DJ playing Holiday songs, characters, a midnight toast and more. Pricing is $99 for adults and $45 for children. A lobby party, without the buffet, is $60 and $35.
• *Portofino Bay Hotel* holds a New Year's Party with multiple food stations, a kids' buffet, complimentary wines, holiday tunes, a midnight toast and more. This is $145 per adult and $35 per child.

At the time of writing, details for the 2016 Holiday season are not yet available. However, Universal Orlando Resort has been very consistent with its Holiday season over the years, and we expect all these events to take place again in 2016.

2016 will be the first Holiday season for *Sapphire Falls Resort*; we expect events similar to the other hotels to take place but no announcement has been made at this time.

Touring Plans

In order to make the most of your time at the parks, we highly recommend you follow one of our touring plans. These touring plans are not designed in order for you to have a leisurely, slow day through the parks; they are designed to get as much accomplished as possible, while still having fun.

How to use our Touring Plans

Touring Plans may mean crossing the park back and forth to save you from being in long queue lines, but ultimately it means you can get the most out of your Universal Orlando Resort experience.

Generally speaking, our touring plans have you riding the most popular attractions (with the longest waits) at the start and end of the day when they are less busy; during the middle of the day, you will be visiting the attractions that have consistent wait times, and shows. This enables you to maximize your time.

Touring with an Express Pass:
These touring plans presume you do not have Express Passes. If you do have these, then you are free to explore the park in whatever order you want, as you won't have to worry about waiting in the queue lines.

If you have an Express Pass, you should do the attractions that do not offer Express Pass (notably *Harry Potter's Forbidden Journey* and *Escape from Gringotts*), first or last in the day.

Touring without an Express Pass:
At the moment, the Universal Orlando theme parks do not have an abundance of attractions and wait times can be long throughout both parks. It is, however, perfectly possible to do all the rides in a single park on the same day with some planning.

We recommend you spend at least one day at each theme park, and then use a third or fourth day to re-do your favorite attractions at both parks, as well as any others you may have missed.

The key to making the most of these touring plans is to arrive at the park before it opens; that means being at the parking garages at least about 60 minutes before park opening if you are driving in. The parking garages open 90 minutes before the first park opens.

If you want to buy tickets on the day, you will need to be at the park gates at least 45 minutes before opening. Otherwise, make sure to be at the park gates at least 30 minutes before opening with your park admission in hand. This is because park gates regularly open up to 30 minutes before the official stated opening time.

Using this Touring Plan:
Follow the steps in order. If there is a particular attraction you do not wish to experience, simply skip that step and then follow the next one - do not change the order of the steps.

1-Day Plan for Universal Studios Florida

Step 1: Be at the turnstiles with your park ticket in hand at least 30 minutes before the park opening time. Proceed through the gates. Grab a park map and head towards *Despicable Me: Minion Mayhem*. Ride it. If the wait is longer than 30 minutes, we would skip this ride as the time you lose here really impacts your day.

Step 2: Experince *Transformers: The Ride*. There is a Single Rider line. If you find that the queue is already very long, then we suggest you skip this step and ride *Transformers* at the end of the day.

Step 3: Ride *Hollywood Rip Ride Rockit*. There is a Single Rider line available, though it moves slowly. At this time of the day, the regular stand by queue line shouldn't be too long anyway. Lockers are required for loose items.

Step 4: Ride *Revenge of the Mummy*. Lockers are required for loose items. A Single Rider line is available. We recommend the standard queue for the theming. Wait times rarely exceed 45 minutes.

Step 5: Experience *The Simpsons Ride*.

Step 6: Ride *Men in Black: Alien Attack*. A Single Rider line is available, which moves quickly. Lockers are required for loose items.

Step 7: Have a Quick Service lunch to maximize your time.

Step 8: Watch *Universal's Superstar Parade*. It is not as popular as Disney's parades; you can get a good spot just minutes before the it starts.

Step 9: Ride *E.T. Adventure*. Waits are usually not more than 30 minutes.

Step 10: Watch *Universal's Horror Make Up Show*. This is our favorite live show a. The theatre is fairly small so arrive about 20 minutes before the performance is due to start to be guaranteed a seat.

Step 11: Watch *Terminator 2: 3D...A Battle Across Time*. This is our other favorite live show at Universal, and is very different to the *Horror Make Up Show*.

Step 12: See *Shrek 4D*.

Step 13: Head to *The Wizarding World of Harry Potter: Diagon Alley*. You want to enter this area at least 3 hours before park closing. Crowds are at the end of the day. Ride *Harry Potter and the Escape from Gringotts*, followed by a return journey on the *Hogwarts Express* (a Park-to-Park ticket is required to ride this). If you have the time, experience *Ollivander's Wand Shop*.

Step 14: Watch the *Universal Cinematic Spectacular*. The area in front of TRANSFORMERS is our favourite spot. Do not be too worried about missing the *Cinematic Spectacular* to get entry into *Diagon Alley* and its attractions.

Note: We do not include all park attractions here due to time constraints. Some attractions target young children such as *Barney* and *Woody Woodpecker* and may not be the most fun for your party.

If you have no interest in *The Wizarding World of Harry Potter*, it is possible to do almost every other attraction in the park in one day.

1-Day Plan for Islands of Adventure

Due to the popularity of *The Wizarding World of Harry Potter: Hogsmeade* many guidebooks are recommending you visit this area early in the day - DON'T! This is what everyone is doing, which means that you end up getting yourself into insanely long queue lines!

The exception to this is if you have Early Entry into *Hogsmeade* – then you should, of course, explore all of *Hogsmeade* during this first hour, and then follow the touring plan below.

Step 1: Be at the park entry turnstiles with your ticket in hand at least 30 minutes before park opening. Proceed through the turnstiles once they start operating. Grab a park map, head straight through the arch and through the *Port of Entry area* of the park. You can come back to explore this beautiful area later in the day.

Step 2: When you reach the end of the path you must turn either left or right. Turn left and cross the bridge under *The Incredible Hulk Coaster*. Turn right and ride *The*

Amazing Adventures of Spider-Man. Lockers are not required for this attraction. Do this before riding *The Hulk* as lines for *Spider-Man* build up more quickly, whereas the Hulk's stay reasonably constant throughout the day.

Step 3: Ride *The Incredible Hulk Coaster*. Lockers are required for loose items.

Step 4: Ride *Dr. Doom's Fearfall*. Lockers are required for loose items.

Step 5: If all has gone to plan, you should have done all this within the first 45 to 60 minutes of your day.

Important: In order to make the most of this touring plan you will now have to make a decision. Choose either to visit kids rides (Step 6 and 7) or do water rides

(Step 8).

Step 6: Cross the park to the *Seuss Landing* area. Ride *The Cat in the Hat*. Lockers are not required for this attraction.

Step 7: Ride *One Fish, Two Fish, Red Fish, Blue Fish*. Be prepared to get wet.

Step 8: Now prepare to get absolutely drenched. Head to the *Toon Lagoon* area and hit the three water rides just before lunch. *Dudley's Do-Right's Ripsaw Falls* should be first, followed by *Popeye & Bluto's Bilge-Rat Barges*, and finally *Jurassic Park River Adventure*.

You will be soaking wet before lunch but most people do these rides after lunch, so you have saved yourself a lot of valuable time in the afternoon. We advise eating somewhere outdoors, away from the air-conditioning.

Step 9: Have lunch. In the interests of time we recommend that you dine at a Quick Service location.

Step 10: If you fit the very limited ride requirements, ride *Pteranodon Flyers*. This will most likely be one of the lengthiest waits of the day.

Step 11: Head to *Seuss Landing* and ride the *High in the Sky Seuss Trolley Train Ride*. This ride can also be prone to long waits.

Step 12: Ride the *Caro-seuss-el*. The wait for this should rarely be above 10 minutes.

Step 13: Experience the shows: *Poseidon's Fury* and *The Eighth Voyage of Sindbad Stunt Show*. If the *Mystic Fountain* is entertaining guests, enjoy that too.

Step 14: Ride *Skull Island: Reign of Kong*. Waits will not be at their shortest of the day but they will be significantly shorter than earlier.

Step 15: Now you only have a few minor rides left to do, as well as *The Wizarding*

World of Harry Potter: Hogsmeade. If there are three hours until park closing or more, follow the next steps in order. If there are less than 3 hours, you may want to head to *The Wizarding World* and follow this touring plan from step number 19.

Step 16: Watch *Oh, the Stories You'll Hear* in *Seuss Landing*.

Step 17: Explore *Camp Jurassic* near *Pteranodon Flyers*.

Step 18: Ride *Storm Force Accelatron*.

Step 19: Head to T*he Wizarding World of Harry Potter: Hogsmeade*. Ride *Dragon Challenge*. This should have almost no wait at this time of day. Lockers are required.

Step 20: Ride *Flight of the Hippogriff*.

Step 21: Have dinner. We recommend *Three Broomsticks* right here in the *Wizarding World*.

Step 22: Experience *Ollivander's Wand Shop*. If you will be visiting *Universal Studios Florida*, skip this as they have a clone of this attraction at *Diagon Alley* with much shorter wait times.

Step 23: Ride *Harry Potter and the Forbidden Journey*. Lockers are required for loose items. As long as you are in line even one minute before the park closes they will let you experience the ride.

Chances are that within the last hour of the park being open, queue lines for most things throughout the park will be very low and *Forbidden Journey* is often a walk-on at this point of the day with no wait in line.

Top Tip: A common theme park trick is to keep the posted wait times higher than they really are during the last operating hour to trick you into not queuing up for rides. Use your judgment. If the park looks less busy now than it did in the middle of the day, then it follows that the waits will be much shorter.

Important: Queue lines usually shut at park closing time. However, if the wait times are extremely long (1 hour+), these may shut early. Ask Team Members at an attraction towards the end of the day if they will close early.

Best of Both Parks in 1-Day Touring Plan

In this touring plan we show you how to hit the biggest attractions in both parks. It is not feasible to do all the attractions at the two parks in just one day, so we have listed the must-dos here.

Remember that you will need a Universal Orlando Park-to-Park ticket to access both parks on the same day.

Doing the best of both parks in one day has become much more difficult since the addition of *The Wizarding World of Harry Potter: Diagon Alley*, due to its immense popularity and the extra guests this has brought to the Universal Orlando Resort.

On extremely busy days, it is unlikely that you will be able to accomplish everything in this plan.

This touring plan assumes high crowds and that the parks are open until at least 9:00pm. The plan also works for lower crowds and shorter opening hours.

Note: If you have Early Park Access such as guests staying at on-site hotels, ride *Escape from Gringotts* first and then pick up the plan from Step 1 and *Despicable Me*. If you want to ride the *Hogwart's Express*, do so towards the end of the day.

Step 1: Be at the turnstiles of *Universal Studios Florida* with your ticket in hand before park opening. Be there at least 30 minutes before the park is set to open, as queues build quickly. Proceed through the turnstiles, grab a park map, head straight ahead and ride *Despicable Me*.

Step 2: Experience *Transformers: The Ride*. Use the Single Rider line to save time if you can.

Step 3: Ride *Hollywood Rip Ride Rockit*. Use the Single Rider queue line to save time if you can. You have now ridden three of the rides with the longest waits in this park.

Step 4: Ride *Revenge of the Mummy*.

Step 5: Lunch - we recommend *Monsters' Cafe* if you are staying in *Universal Studios Florida* and want a quick meal. Having a Table Service meal will undermine this entire plan.

Step 6: Now it is time to make your way over to *Universal's Islands of Adventure*. Be prepared for long queue lines as this is the busiest point in the day - however lines will still generally be shorter than at *Universal Studios Florida*, which is why we started there first.

Step 7: Ride *The Incredible Hulk Coaster*. There is a Single Rider line available.

Step 8: If it is past 3:00pm, we recommend you skip this step. Otherwise, choose one of the following water attractions. Ride *Dudley Do-Right's Ripsaw Falls*, *Popeye & Bluto's Bilge-Rat Barges* or *Jurassic Park River Adventure*.

Step 9: Ride T*he Amazing Adventures of Spider-Man*. The queue will be long at this time of day. Use the Single Rider line if possible to save time.

Step 11: If *Skull Island: Reign of Kong* has opened by the time of your visit, ride this attraction now.

Step 12: Explore *The Wizarding World of Harry Potter: Hogsmeade*. The crowds will probably have lightened by now.

Ride *Dragon Challenge*, which should not have a wait longer than 30 minutes, especially at this point in the day.

Step 13: Ride *Harry Potter and the Forbidden Journey*. The line should be substantially smaller than it is in the morning.

Step 14: Catch the *Hogwarts Express* over to *Diagon Alley*. If you are boarding the train 30 minutes or sooner before the park officially closes you will have to move quickly to make it to the final ride.

Step 15: Proceed to *Escape from Gringotts*. This ride may have

a long queue, but it should be at the lowest it has been all day.

As long as you are in the queue line before park closing you will be able to ride, except in periods of extremely high crowds where the queue line may close earlier.

If time still remains, have dinner somewhere in the *Wizarding World* or elsewhere in the park.

The Future

The future of the Universal Orlando Resort looks bright with several projects currently in the works. In this section we cover what you can look forward to at the resort in the coming months and years.

In September 2013, Universal's President and Chief Executive Officer, Steve Burke, announced at a conference that Universal plans to open one new attraction per year for the foreseeable future. This is a pace that no other major theme park resort can match, and sets an exciting precedent for the future.

Volcano Bay Water Park – 2017

Universal Orlando Resort has ambitious plans to expand, and rival the Walt Disney World Resort, including by building its very own highly-themed water park.

Universal already owns the land on which *Wet 'n Wild* water park sits, but it does not have its own on-site water park with integrated tickets, room charging and other facilities. Wet 'n' Wild will be closing at the end of 2016, and the new water park – Volcano Bay – will open in 2017. This will be on-site and better themed than *Wet 'n' Wild*.

The park will measure about 30 acres, which is comparable to the size of *Wet 'n Wild*, and half of the size of one of Walt Disney World's water parks. The park is being built on a plot of land south of *Cabana Bay Beach Resort*, with the central icon being a "massive, 200-foot erupting volcano".

Universal Orlando says this water park will feature "radically-innovative attractions, peaceful moments of relaxation and an experience that we hope will change the way guests think about water theme parks."

No exact opening date has been given but Universal has said it will be open "by June 1, 2017".

Fast and Furious: Supercharged – 2018

A new *Fast & Furious: Supercharged* attraction will be making its way to *Universal Studios Florida* in 2018. This attraction will be located in the San Francisco area of the park. The two previous attractions in this area – *Beetlejuice* and *Disaster*, have closed to make way for this new ride.

Universal says: "This ride is going to fuse everything you love about the films with an original storyline and incredible ride technology. You'll get to check out some of the high-speed, supercharged cars you've seen on the big screen. You'll be immersed in the underground racing world made famous in the films and explore the headquarters of Toretto and his team. Then, you'll board specially-designed vehicles for an adrenaline-pumping ride with your favorite stars."

We expect this new attraction to be similar to the Fast & Furious attraction at *Universal Studios Hollywood*, which consists of a tram filled with guests and a wraparound 3D screen with a chase sequence as your tram moves in time with it.

Cabana Bay Beach Resort Expansion – 2017

Universal Orlando has announced that their Prime Value resort – *Cabana Bay* will be expanded to allow more guests to stay on-site at their most affordable rooms. The expansion will add 400 guest rooms in two new towers. Some of these rooms will have amazing views of Universal's Volcano Bay water park.

Jimmy Fallon Attraction – 2017

Another new attraction, called *Race Through New York: Starring Jimmy Fallon*, will be coming to *Universal Studios Florida* in 2017. This attraction replaces *Twister*, which has now closed.

Universal says: "Inspired by the popular Tonight Show segment, this upcoming ride *Race through New York Starring Jimmy Fallon* will pit you against Jimmy in a wild race through one of the world's greatest cities – New York City. Opens in 2017."

"Guests step right into Studio 6B where Jimmy will challenge them. On the adventure, they will twist, turn and laugh as they speed through the streets – and skies – of The Big Apple, encountering everything from iconic landmarks to the deepest subway tunnels, and anything else that comes to Jimmy's mind."

New Nintendo attractions - Confirmed

In May 2015, Universal Parks and Resorts announced a partnership with Nintendo. A Universal Orlando press release says that together both companies will "create spectacular, dedicated experiences based on Nintendo's wildly popular games, characters and worlds"

"The immersive experiences will include major attractions at Universal's theme parks and will feature Nintendo's most famous characters and games."

No specific details have been given as to the franchises that will be coming or an opening date.

And More

Universal Orlando also plans to more than triple the number of on-site hotel rooms to between 10,000 and 15,000 in the future. With a new water park coming and new attractions, they could certainly do with more on-site rooms.

In 2016, Universal also bought large plots of land, which would be more than large enough to create a third and possibly even fourth theme park, as well as hotels. The land that *Wet 'n' Wild* stood on until 2017 will also be empty.

It looks like the next three to five years could be filled with announcements that could mean that Universal Orlando Resort will soon rival Walt Disney World in scope and offerings.

A Special Thanks

Thank you very much for reading *The Independent Guide to Universal Orlando 2017*. We hope this travel guide has made a big difference to your vacation and you have found some tips that will save you time, money and hassle.

To get in touch with any feedback or questions, please use the 'Contact Us' section of our website at www.independentguidebooks.com/contact-us/.

To stay up to date on all the latest developments and updates be sure to like our Facebook page at www.facebook.com/independentguidebooks and on Twitter @indepguides. You can also sign up to our newsletter on our website (on the right sidebar).

If you have enjoyed this guide you will want to check out:
* The Independent Guide to Walt Disney World 2017
* The Independent Guide to Universal Studios Hollywood 2017
* The Independent Guide to Disneyland 2017
* The Independent Guide to Disneyland Paris 2017
* The Independent Guide to Paris 2017
* The Independent Guide to New York City 2017
* The Independent Guide to London 2017
* The Independent Guide to Dubai 2017
* The Independent Guide to Hong Kong 2017

Our theme park guide books give you detailed information on every ride, show and attraction and insider tips that will save you hours of waiting in queue lines! Our city guides are great overviews of fascinating metropolis' with top attractions, good places to eat and stay, explanations of the transport system and much more.

Have fun at the Universal Orlando Resort!

Photo credits:
The following photos have been used in this guide under a Creative Commons attribution 2.0 license:
Universal Globe - Alison Sanfacon; Photos of all on-site hotels, Hollywood Rip Ride Rocket, Jimmy Fallon, Fast and Furious, Shrek 4-D, Reign of Kong, Spider-Man, Nightlife/Rising Star, CityWalk Dining/Cowfish, Mini Golf, Universal Dining Plan/Antojitos, Tri-Wizard Tournament, Blue Man Group and Rock the Universe, - Universal Orlando; Men in Black, Woody Woodpecker's Nuthouse Coaster, One Fish Two Fish, Storm Force Accelatron, Pteranodon Flyers and Single Rider - Jeremy Thompson; Animal Actors on Location, Planning/WDW Cast Member and Express Pass, Character Meets with Sideshow Bob - Theme Park Tourist; Chad Sparks - Hogwarts Express; Q-Bot - accesso. com; Refillable Mug - Universal Orlando Blog; Nintendo Logo - Nintendo Co., Ltd.
Cover Images: Hulk - Dave Walker, Springfield - 'osseous', Dinosaur - Theme Park Tourist, IOA Panorama - John M

HARRY POTTER, characters, names and related indicia are trademarks of and © Warner Bros. Entertainment Inc. Harry Potter Publishing Rights © JKR.

Universal Studios Florida

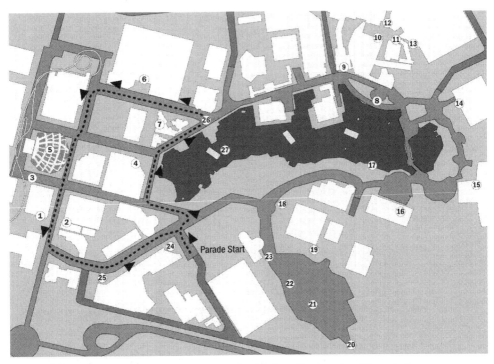

PRODUCTION CENTRAL
1. Despicable Me: Minion Mayhem
2. Shrek 4-D (Express)
3. Hollywood Rip Ride Rockit (Express)
4. 'TRANSFORMERS' The Ride: 3D (Express)
5. Music Plaza Stage

NEW YORK
6. Revenge of the Mummy (Express)
7. The Blue Brothers Show

THE WIZARDING WORLD OF HARRY POTTER - DIAGON ALLEY
8. The Knight Bus
9. Hogwart's Express - King's Cross Station
10. Knockturn Alley
11. Ollivanders
12. Harry Potter and the Escape from Gringotts
13. Live Performances

WORLD EXPO

14. Fear Factor Live (Express)
15. MEN IN BLACK: Alien Attack (Express)
16. The Simpsons Ride (Express)
17. Kang & Kodos' Twirl & Hurl

WOODY WOODPECKER'S KIDZONE
18. Animal Actor's On Location! (Express)
19. A Day in the Park with Barney (Express)
20. Curious George Goes To Town
21. Woody Woodpecker's Nuthouse Coaster (Express)
22. Fievel's Playland
23. E.T. Adventure (Express)

HOLLYWOOD
24. Universal Orlando's Horror Make-Up Show (Express)
25. TERMINATOR 2: 3-D (Express)

PARADE ROUTE
26. Universal's Superstar Parade

PARK-WIDE ENTERTAINMENT
27. Universal's Cinematic Spectacular

Islands of Adventure

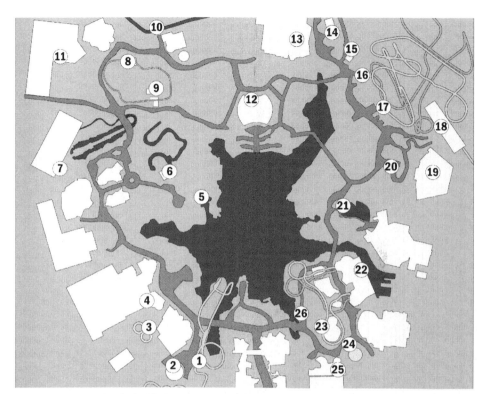

MARVEL SUPER HERO ISLAND
1. The Incredible Hulk Coaster (Express)
2. Storm Force Accelatron (Express)
3. Doctor Doom's Fear Fall (Express)
4. The Amazing Adventures of Spider-Man (Express)

TOON LAGOON
5. Me Ship, The Olive
6. Popeye & Bluto's Bilge-Rat Barges (Express)
7. Dudley Do-Right's Ripsaw Falls (Express)

JURASSIC PARK
8. Pteranodon Flyers
9. Camp Jurassic
10. Jurassic Park River Adventure (Express)
11. Skull Island: Reign of Kong
12. Jurassic Park Discovery Center

THE WIZARDING WORLD OF HARRY POTTER - HOGSMEADE
13. Harry Potter and the Forbidden Journey
14. Flight of the Hippogriff (Express)
15. Live Performances
16. Ollivanders
17. Dragon Challenge (Express)
18. Hogwarts Express - Hogsmeade Station

THE LOST CONTINENT
19. The Eighth Voyage of Sindbad Stunt Show (Express)
20. The Mystic Fountain
21. Poseidon's Fury (Express)

SEUSS LANDING
22. The High in the Sky Seuss Trolley Train Ride! (Express)
23. Caro-Seuss-El (Express)
24. One Fish, Two Fish, Red Fish, Blue Fish (Express)
25. The Cat in The Hat (Express)
26. If I Ran the Zoo

Made in the USA
Lexington, KY
28 November 2016